O WORSHIP THE KING

Hymns of Assurance and Praise to Encourage Your Heart

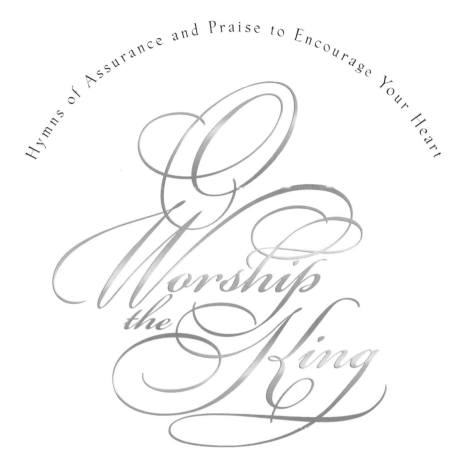

O Worship the King

JOHN MACARTHUR

JONI EARECKSON TADA

ROBERT & BOBBIE WOLGEMUTH

CROSSWAY BOOKS • WHEATON, ILLINOIS
A DIVISION OF GOOD NEWS PUBLISHERS

O Worship the King

Copyright © 2000 by John MacArthur, Joni Eareckson Tada, and Robert and Bobbie Wolgemuth

Published by Crossway Books
A division of Good News Publishers
1300 Crescent Street
Wheaton, Illinois 60187

Design: Cindy Kiple

First printing, 2000
Printed in the United States of America
ISBN 1-58134-268-3 special edition
Hymn quotations are taken from *Trinity Hymnal,* revised edition, copyright ©1990 by Great Commission Publications, Inc., Suwanee, GA.

The music reprinted at the back of this book is taken from *Trinity Hymnal,* revised edition, copyright © 1990 by Great Commission Publications, Inc. Used by permission.

The music for "Be Thou My Vision" is from *The Church Hymnary.* Harmonization by David Evans (1874-1948). © Oxford University Press. 3 Park Road, London, England NW1 6XN. Used by permission.

Scripture taken from the *Holy Bible: New International Version*®. copyright © 1973, 1978, 1984 by International Bible Society. Used by permission of Zondervan Publishing House. All rights reserved.

The "NIV" and "New International Version" trademarks are registered in the United States Patent and Trademark Office by International Bible Society. Use of either trademark requires the permission of International Bible Society.

*To all the saints triumphant who set theology to music
and helped shape my understanding and conviction
through the years as I sang the truth.*

JOHN MACARTHUR

———

*For all the harmony around the campfire at
Rehoboth beach, for the rousing choruses you led
during those cold nights in the farm truck, for all the
times we'd push away our plates and finish dinner
with a hymn . . . thank you, Daddy.*

JONI EARECKSON TADA

———

*To our grandparents who sang hymns in the
potato fields of Lancaster County with their children
while they worked or let us sit on their laps at old upright
pianos, and to our parents and siblings who still love
to belt out the melodies that bind our hearts
together at every family gathering.*

ROBERT & BOBBIE WOLGEMUTH

———

Special Thanks to:

Mr. John Duncan
of TVP Studios, Greenville, SC,
Executive Producer of the musical recording
for *O Worship the King.*

Dr. Paul Plew
Chairman of the Department of Music
at The Master's College,
who directed the musical production.

The students of The Master's Chorale
who contributed their superb singing skills
and love for these hymns to the CD.

We are deeply grateful for the gifts of these friends
and accomplished professionals.

The publisher's share of income from the *O Worship the King* compact disc is being donated by Good News Publishers/Crossway Books to JAF Ministries, the worldwide disability outreach of Joni Eareckson Tada. For more information about JAF Ministries, please write to JAF Ministries, Post Office Box 3333, Agoura Hills, California 91301 or call 818-707-5664 or go to website—www.joniandfriends.org

---

Table of Contents

FOREWORD

Quite an unusual story lies behind the writing of this book. But then we might expect as much because the authors—Joni Eareckson Tada, John MacArthur, and Robert and Bobbie Wolgemuth—are such extraordinary people!

In the broadest sense this book is the story of God's unfailing faithfulness, as told in the great hymns of the faith and in the stories that lie behind these hymns. Whether written in the midst of overwhelming tragedy or in moments of great joy, the hymns of this book have profoundly touched the lives of Christians through the centuries—and they will do so again as these pages are read.

But the immediate story behind this book starts (as many unusual stories do!) with our very dear friend Joni Eareckson Tada. Joni, as you know, broke her neck in a diving accident when she was seventeen years old, and she has lived as a quadriplegic for more than three decades ever since. But by God's grace and through Joni's perseverance, she lives a most extraordinary life—a life that above all else reflects the joy of the Lord. One of my favorite memories, in fact, is stopping with Joni in hotel lobbies to sing impromptu hymns of praise and worship—to the delight and sometimes wonder of other hotel guests.

The occasion that gave birth to this book and the accompanying CD, then, was *Joni's idea*—this time to sing "impromptu hymns" with Dr. John MacArthur at the Good News-Crossway 60th Anniversary Banquet, in the summer of 1998. The theme for the banquet was "Celebrating Sixty Years of God's Faithfulness," and both Joni and John MacArthur, Joni's pastor and close friend, were scheduled to speak. Joni and John checked with me first to be sure it was okay—and of course Joni doesn't take "no" for an answer! But it came as a complete surprise to everyone else when Joni invited John to join her on the platform to sing an "impromptu" duet of their favorite hymns.

Rarely have I seen an audience so deeply moved. As they listened to Joni sing the praises of God's faithfulness, it was a remarkable moment—a moment when we were all given a glimpse of God's glory.

Immediately after the banquet I started urging John and Joni to make a CD of hymns. And from there the ideas just kept growing. Joni invited her friends Robert and Bobbie Wolgemuth to join in since, as Joni noted, "We've sung together for years . . . over the telephone, in hotel lobbies, in restaurant parking lots, and they'd love to be part of this." And of course we'd need a book to go with the CD. But there are so many great hymns, we'll really need *four* books!

Just recently all these ideas came together in a most exciting way. The recording studio was booked; John MacArthur brought Dr. Paul Plew and the highly acclaimed Chorale of Master's College; and Joni, John, Robert, and Bobbie joined in singing twelve of the greatest hymns of all time. As Joni reflected later, "The adventure of singing together was pure delight. It was two solid days of worship and praise."

Now, almost two years after Joni "cooked up" her idea for a duet, her idea has come to life in this book and the CD tucked into the front cover. It is our prayer that through this book and CD you will also see a glimpse of God's glory and discover a deeper understanding of His faithfulness, and that you would join with Joni and John and Robert and Bobbie—and indeed the Church of our Lord Jesus Christ through the centuries—in singing the praises of our Lord and Savior.

O worship the King all-glorious above,
O gratefully sing, his power and his love.

Lane T. Dennis, Ph.D.
Publisher

INTRODUCTION

The year was 1735. John Wesley was making his way across the Atlantic from his homeland in England. He and several dozen other travelers were aboard the three-masted merchant schooner named *Simmonds*. But halfway between the British Isles and the Georgia shore, the ship encountered a mighty storm.

The sailors dropped the sails and ordered the passengers to hang on for their very lives. Gale force winds pounded the craft mercilessly. Huge waves crashed over the decks. The timbers of the boat groaned as the storm relentlessly punished her. Everyone—even the most seasoned of the sailors—was terrified.

But in the midst of the tempest, Wesley heard something. At first, he thought it might be music, but under the circumstances, the thought of such a thing seemed highly unlikely—even outrageous.

Amazingly, what John Wesley found was a group of Moravian Christians, gathered together, singing hymns. Although they were certainly afraid like the others, their spirits were lifted by the sounds of praise coming from their own lips. Imagine hearing the sound above the din—the singing of hymns calming fearful hearts.

In the New Testament we read the account of Paul and Silas, chained together in a Philippian jail. Although much different than the turbulence of a vicious Atlantic storm, there could have been the same kind of hopelessness in the hearts of these men. So what did they do? They sang hymns. Can you imagine the breathtaking beauty of the harmonic strains of two men's voices, piercing the midnight despair of a prison? These men had no idea what was to become of them at daybreak. But the singing of hymns calmed their fearful hearts and lifted their spirits.

Most Christians know the words to *The Doxology*. It's often sung in churches when the filled offering plates are brought to the front of the sanctuary.

Praise God from whom all blessings flow,
Praise Him all creatures here below.
Praise Him above ye heavenly host.
Praise Father, Son, and Holy Ghost.

This time, the familiar strains of *The Doxology* were quietly wafting from an unlikely place. This was no church. This was the visitor's dugout at the Oakland Stadium. It was October 1988, the fifth game of the World Series. Just before this moment, a young athlete named Orel Hershiser had pitched another shutout inning against the Oakland A's. Over the past few weeks he and his Los Angeles Dodger teammates had clinched the National League pennant with a dramatic seven-game series victory over the New York Mets. Orel had been named the Most Valuable Player and now was feeling the pressure of pitching against Jose Conseco, Mark McGwire, and the mighty Oakland A's.

Between visits to the mound, Orel sat quietly in the dugout, his head resting on the concrete block wall directly behind the bench. Closing his eyes, he softly sang praises to his heavenly Father. Ironically, three days later, following the Dodgers' victory over the A's, Orel was on the set of "The Tonight Show with Johnny Carson," singing *The Doxology* to tens of millions of viewers. Once again, an unsuspected hymn-sing calmed a fearful heart and lifted spirits.

Our hope is that reading the stories of these twelve hymns and learning of their biblical roots will inspire you to sing along and to experience God's grace in a new and refreshing way—just as we experienced in preparing this book and CD.

And there may be times when these hymns, like the sounds coming from the storm-tossed ship, the dank halls of a Philippian jail, and the dugout of a baseball stadium, will calm your fears and lift your spirits.

This is our prayer for you.

Joni Eareckson Tada, Agoura Hills, California

John MacArthur, Sun Valley, California

Robert & Bobbie Wolgemuth, Orlando, Florida

A Mighty Fortress Is Our God

MARTIN LUTHER

(1483-1546)

A mighty fortress is our God, a bulwark never failing;

our helper he amid the flood of mortal ills prevailing.

For still our ancient foe doth seek to work us woe;

his craft and power are great; and armed with cruel hate,

on earth is not his equal.

Did we in our own strength confide, our striving would be losing;

were not the right man on our side, the man of God's own choosing.

Dost ask who that may be? Christ Jesus it is he,

Lord Sabaoth his name, from age to age the same,

and he must win the battle.

And though this world, with devils filled, should threaten to undo us,

we will not fear, for God hath willed his truth to triumph through us.

The prince of darkness grim, we tremble not for him;

his rage we can endure, for lo! His doom is sure;

one little word shall fell him.

That Word above all earthly pow'rs, no thanks to them, abideth;

the Spirit and the gifts are ours through him who with us sideth.

Let goods and kindred go, this mortal life also;

the body they may kill: God's truth abideth still;

his kingdom is forever.

AT THE HEART OF THE HYMN

Robert Wolgemuth

❧

*L*ET'S SAY YOU'RE ON A GUIDED TOUR of the French countryside. You are riding in a bus, and the tour director is describing the landscape from a microphone in the front. The driver turns your bus down a long, tree-lined road that leads to a castle . . . one more castle. Frankly, you'd rather be back in the hotel. It's been a long day of sightseeing and, with all due respect to the ingenious castle-builders of the seventeenth century, the last thing you need is one more sight to see. As you stare blankly out the window, you don't actually see anything. In fact, as the guide describes the details of the scene, including each intricate peculiarity of this citadel, you don't hear anything either. You close your eyes and try to sleep.

Now let's roll the calendar back a few decades—time travel. It's the early forties. You find yourself on that very same wooded lane, headed toward the identical castle. But this time you're not on a bus. Even though lots of other folks are crammed into this vehicle, it's actually a military personnel carrier. The voice coming from the front is your commanding officer. What he's describing to you is the location you and your fellow soldiers are going to be using the next day as a battleground. The castle has been secured as your stronghold, and your company will be returning to this same place on foot tonight.

You're completely exhausted from the rigorous activities of the day. But you're not sleepy. In fact, you've never been so awake in your life. You study the trees, looking for potential hiding places for enemy soldiers. You scan the castle, considering which locations would be suitable for you to use as you watch the movements of the opposition. Your very life could depend on your careful attention to this moment, and you know it.

Our struggle is not against flesh and blood,

but against the rulers, against the authorities,

against the powers of this dark world

and against the spiritual forces

of evil in the heavenly realms.

Ephesians 6:12

When our two daughters were old enough to carry a tune, Bobbie asked them to join her on the piano bench. She opened a hymnal to this Martin Luther classic and taught the girls every verse. Of course, it took more than one sitting, but soon they had mastered every word of every verse—including the word "bulwark."

One day Missy stopped singing. "What's a bulwark?" she asked.

"A fortress," Bobbie responded. "It's a place where people can go to protect themselves from their enemies. A bulwark is a strong, safe place—like a castle." Missy seemed satisfied and continued to sing.

For the next few years Bobbie and I talked about the idea of a bulwark. Sometimes we found ourselves blankly staring out our parenting "window," glassy-eyed from the rigors of the day-to-day. But then we'd remind each other that life was not a prepackaged bus tour but a daily—and extremely unpredictable and dangerous—confrontation with the very forces of darkness. Life was spiritual warfare.

Until Missy and Julie left our home to establish their own, we sat together in church every Sunday. When the hymn selection was number 92, we'd look at each other with a knowing smile. And without so much as even touching the hymnal in the pew rack in front of us, we'd stand and sing every verse from memory.

A mighty fortress is our God, a bulwark never failing.

There is a war going on. But our Castle never fails.

IN THE LIGHT OF THE WORD

John MacArthur

HIS BEST-KNOWN AND MOST ENDURING HYMN from the early Protestant Reformation celebrates the utter invincibility of almighty God—and in particular the safety He affords those who take refuge in Him. It begins with a powerful statement echoing Psalm 46:1, "God is our refuge and strength."

By the end of the first stanza, however, the focus of the hymn is on "our ancient foe," the devil. No doubt many careless singers have belted out the closing phrase of the first stanza (" . . . on earth is not his equal") as if it were a line of praise about God. But Satan, not God, is the subject here. He is, after all, the believer's arch-adversary. It is fitting that a hymn about God as our stronghold should consider what kind of a threat Satan poses to the security of that stronghold.

Some have suggested that Luther had an obsession with the devil. A well-known legend has Luther heaving an ink-pot across the room at Satan. Supposedly, the ink-stain is still visible on a wall in Wartburg Castle today (though most researchers believe the ink-stain was deliberately applied to the wall long after Luther's time in order to substantiate the popular legend). In figurative terms, Luther certainly did throw a printer's ink-pot at the devil, with his translation of Scripture into the language of the people and with his own voluminous writings, including this favorite hymn.

It is an undeniable fact that Luther was constantly haunted with a vivid awareness of Satan's opposition. Luther spoke often of how the devil would awaken him at night to accuse him, argue with him, or tempt him. To Luther, the devil posed a far more present danger than the flesh-and-blood adversaries he contended with.

But Luther never wrote of Satan's fierce power and opposition without also stressing the still greater power of God and the certainty of the devil's destruction. The third stanza of this hymn is a classic example. Here Luther also highlights the absolute ease with which God's power will overthrow both Satan and a world full of his evil minions. "One little word" from the Lord's lips will be their undoing.

Modern song leaders sometimes shorten hymns by leaving out a verse or singing only the first and last stanzas. That approach doesn't work at all with "A Mighty Fortress," because one stanza builds upon another with a continuity that runs from the first verse through the last. For example, the phrase "one little word shall fell him" comes at the end of the third stanza; and the opening words of the fourth speak of "That Word." The reference makes no sense if the third stanza is omitted. A similar progression of thought ties all the stanzas together, so that the hymn must be sung in full to make sense.

The hymn is filled with rich theology and biblical references. For example, the second stanza speaks in these terms of the One who assures our ultimate victory:

> *Dost ask who that may be?*
> *Christ Jesus, it is he,*
> *Lord Sabaoth, his Name,*
> *From age to age the same,*
> *And he must win the battle.*

"Lord Sabaoth" is an expression used in Romans 9:29 and James 5:4 ("Lord Almighty"). "Sabaoth" is a transliteration of the Hebrew word meaning "hosts" or "armies." Literally, then, this applies a familiar Old Testament title for God, "Lord of Hosts," to Jesus Christ. Both the use of this name and the phrase "from age to age the same" (cf. Isaiah 51:8) are powerful affirmations of the deity of Christ.

The triumphant final verse of the hymn distills the message of the whole: The worst that the enemies of truth can do is really nothing. They are all perishing. But the Lord, His kingdom, and all those who belong to Him will endure forever. And so the hymn closes as it began, with an echo of Psalm 46: "Therefore we will not fear, though the earth give way and the mountains fall into the heart of the sea.... The Lord Almighty is with us; the God of Jacob is our fortress" (vv. 2, 11).

FROM OUT OF THE PAST
Bobbie Wolgemuth

*I*NSTEAD OF ENTERING THE PRACTICE OF CIVIL LAW, this well-educated son of a magistrate entered a convent of Augustinian monks when he was twenty-two years old. Because a close friend had been killed and Luther himself had been struck by lightning, Luther withdrew from the world of business to find some answers. Those answers came from the pages of a Latin Bible, which he eventually distilled into the doctrine of justification by faith. At twenty-four he became a priest and acquired such a great reputation for wisdom that he was asked to be a professor at the University of Wittenberg in Germany. His desire to increase his knowledge of the truth and to prepare the minds of others to receive it was insatiable.

At the age of thirty-four, Martin encountered a Dominican friar who proclaimed that anyone who would pay a certain sum of money would be granted special favors for his soul and the souls of his friends. When the cleric promised, "The moment the money tinkles in the chest, your father's soul mounts up out of purgatory," Martin was shocked at the blasphemy. On October 31, 1517, he posted 95 theses or complaints against the practices of the Roman Catholic Church on the doors of the Cathedral of Wittenberg. He wrote and preached that Christ alone provides redemption and salvation, that the knowledge of the Scriptures should be reestablished, and that congregational singing should be a part of the worship and instruction of the people. Crowds rallied around him in agreement until his friends began to warn him of the severe dangers of contending against the Pope.

His answer to them was, "I protest that property, reputation, and honors shall all be of no estimation with me, compared with the defense of the truth. I have only a frail body to lose. If, in obedience to God, I lose it through violence or fraud, what is the loss of a few hours of life? Sufficient for me is the lovely Redeemer and Advocate, My Lord Jesus Christ, to whose praise I will sing as long as I live."

The body they may kill, God's truth abideth still:
His kingdom is forever

Two years later the Pope issued a warrant for his arrest and the burning of all his writings. Luther, however, continued to write, declaring that the Word of God was the most legitimate weapon to combat error.

Though the Bible had for centuries been locked away from the majority, now all of Germany was being illumined. When Luther stepped out of a carriage in Worms, Germany, to meet his accusers, he exclaimed, "God will be on my side. Christ lives, and I will enter Worms though all the gates of Hell and all the powers of darkness oppose."

Did we in our own strength confide,
Our striving would be losing;

Were not the right man on our side,

The Man of God's own choosing.

Dost ask who that may be? Christ Jesus, it is he.

Lovers of truth were inspired, and his writings were translated all over Europe. Disciples were so enlightened and determined to fight for the truth that the rage of persecutions became more violent. If a man uttered a word against the Roman Church, he was seized. If in the privacy of their own cottage parents read the Bible or taught their children the Ten Commandments, the Lord's Prayer, or the Apostles' Creed, it was considered a criminal act sufficient to bring the offenders to the stake. It was reported from Brussels that two disciples were burned at the stake and were heard singing in alternate response, "*Te Deum laudamus*" ("We praise Thee, O God").

Declaring music to be second only to the Word of God, Luther composed sacred hymns so that "the Word of God may dwell among the people also by means of song." He exclaimed that music "is a gift and grace of God, not an invention of men. Thus it drives out the Devil and makes people cheerful." As a means of warfare, Luther proclaimed that "the Devil, the originator of sorrowful anxieties and restless troubles, flees before the sound of music almost as much as before the Word of God."

"A Mighty Fortress Is Our God" became the battle cry for the Reformers as they endured suffering for their radical belief in a personal and biblical faith in Jesus Christ alone. Based on Psalm 46, the hymn has been translated into languages all over the world and continues to be a source of strength and encouragement to believers everywhere.

It is Well With My Soul

HORATIO G. SPAFFORD

1828-1888

When peace, like a river, attendeth my way,
when sorrows like sea billows roll;
whatever my lot, thou hast taught me to say,
"It is well, it is well with my soul."

CHORUS:
It is well (It is well)
with my soul; (with my soul)
it is well, it is well with my soul.

Though Satan should buffet, though trials should come,
let this blest assurance control,
that Christ has regarded my helpless estate,
and has shed his own blood for my soul.

CHORUS

My sin—O the bliss of this glorious thought!—
my sin not in part but the whole,
is nailed to the cross and I bear it no more;
praise the Lord, praise the Lord, O my soul!

CHORUS

O Lord, haste the day when the faith shall be sight,
the clouds be rolled back as a scroll,
the trump shall resound and the Lord shall descend,
"Even so"—it is well with my soul.

CHORUS

At the Heart of the Hymn
Joni Eareckson Tada

You will keep in perfect peace him whose mind is
steadfast, because he trusts in you.

—Isaiah 26:3

*I*T WAS ONLY AFTER I GOT OUT of the hospital and wheeled through
the front door of my home that I was hit with the cold hard facts of my paralysis.
Doorways were too narrow. Sinks were too high. My knees hit the edge of the din-
ing table. A plate of food was placed in front of me, but my hands remained limp
in my lap. Someone else, at least for the first few months, fed me. I felt confined
and trapped. Our cozy home had become an adverse and foreign environment.

My confinement forced me to look at another captive. When the apostle Paul
was in a Roman jail, he thanked the believers in Philippi for their concern and
reassured them, "I have learned to be content whatever the circumstances"
(Philippians 4:11).

Paul was talking about an internal quietness of heart, supernaturally given,
that gladly submits to God in all circumstances. Quietness of heart has nothing
to do with prison bars, wheelchairs, or physical hardships. Quietness of heart
has to do with no more peevish thoughts, plotting ways of escape, or vexing
and fretting that only lead to a frantic state of mind. Contentment is a sedate spirit
that is able to keep quiet as it bears up under suffering.

Paul learned how to live this way. "I have learned the secret of being content in
any and every situation" (Philippians 4:12). What was the secret Paul learned? The
Puritan Jeremiah Burroughs said that the New Testament word for contentment carries the idea of sufficiency, as when Paul also wrote, "My [God's] grace is sufficient

for you, for my power is made perfect in weakness" (2 Corinthians 12:9). Paul's secret was simply learning to lean on the Lord Jesus. Paul learned this. It meant making tough choices—deciding this and not that; going this direction and not that one.

In a small way I understand making choices like these. When I finally got tired of being fed, I painstakingly learned how to feed myself with a bent spoon inserted into my arm-splint. It was humiliating to wear a bib and smear apple-sauce all over my clothes. I could have given up—it would have been easy, and many wouldn't have blamed me for quitting. But I had to make a choice. I decided that the awkwardness of feeding myself outweighed the fleeting satisfaction of self-pity. My secret was learning to lean on Jesus and say, "O God, help me with this!" Today I manage a spoon quite well.

I didn't get back the use of my arms or hands. But I did learn to be content.

Christ is not a magic wand that can be waved over our heartaches to make them disappear. As we wrap our hands (or our hearts) around a task and, in faith, learn to follow Him, divine energy surges through us. God's strength works in us at the moment we exercise faith for the task.

He gives you strength to hold your tongue when you feel you have cause for complaining. He imparts the strength to look out for another's interest before your own. He infuses the strength to choose a bright attitude when you wake up in the morning tired. He gives you strength to say, "It is well."

So try it. Or rather, learn it. Learn to sing that same simple note three times, slowly and measured with no breathing in between. "It ... is ... well," and then, "with ... my ... soul." If ever a hymn conveyed in music the perfect peace of learning to be content in Christ and His sufficient grace, it is this one.

When peace, like a river, attendeth my way,
When sorrows like sea billows roll;
Whatever my lot, thou hast taught me to say,

"It is well, it is well with my soul."
It is well with my soul;
It is well, it is well with my soul.

IN THE LIGHT OF THE WORD
John MacArthur

THE POWERFUL EMOTIONS CONVEYED in the music of this song are well-suited to lyrics borne out of deep passion, as these were. And yet amazingly, this is not really a song about subjective feelings and emotions. Instead, the songwriter's focus was on an objective spiritual reality that anchored him at all times—whether he was experiencing "peace, like a river" or whether billowing sorrow overwhelmed him. In the midst of both emotional extremes, his heart and mind returned to the truth that kept him spiritually anchored—the promise that his soul was eternally safe from God's judgment.

The apostle Paul noted that Christians often experience sorrow, but it is nothing like the sorrow of those who have no hope (1 Thessalonians 4:13). We can find comfort in the knowledge that we will enjoy God's abiding blessing and perfect joy throughout all eternity. Therefore, all our earthly sorrows are merely temporary. There is no more comforting assurance in all the world. The soul that truly knows the assurance of such eternal well-being is a soul at peace, even in the midst of life's most devastating and heart-wrenching sorrows.

Job, who suffered as much earthly sorrow as any man has ever borne, took refuge in the hope of future blessing: "I know that my Redeemer lives, and that in the end he will stand upon the earth. And after my skin has been destroyed, yet in my flesh I will see God" (Job 19:25-26).

For Horatio Spafford, in the wake of similar tragedy, the assurance of his soul's well-being was grounded in the same living Redeemer that Job spoke of. Spafford's hope was in Christ, who "shed his own blood" on the believer's behalf. So when Spafford tasted the anguish of human sorrow, his mind turned to the infinite suffering that Christ had already borne on his behalf. That is why in circumstances when most men's minds would have been consumed with self-pity and bitter emotions, Spafford wrote a gospel song of gratitude for Christ's vicarious atonement.

The song is a potent reminder of how every Christian should respond to the vicissitudes of life—particularly life's heartaches. Whatever the source of our sorrows ("Though Satan should buffet, though trials should come"), we can find a powerful comfort in knowing that Christ literally shed His own precious lifeblood for us:

> *If God is for us, who can be against us? He who did not spare his own Son, but delivered him up for us all—how will he not, also, along with him, graciously give us all things?*
>
> —ROMANS 8:31-32

The shedding of Christ's blood was a payment for sin. He made Himself a guilt offering on behalf of sinners (Isaiah 53:10). He bore their sin (vv. 4, 6). He satisfied the righteousness of God and the divine wrath against sin by bearing the iniquities of His people and suffering the penalty for sin in their place (v. 11). That is the doctrine of vicarious atonement, and it is the whole subject of Spafford's third stanza, which is the heart of this song.

Although Spafford's earthly sorrows were an excruciating burden for him, he knew those sorrows were temporary. And that temporal burden served as a poignant reminder that an even greater, eternal burden had been lifted from him by Christ, who took the full guilt of sin and carried that guilt to the cross. Thereby paying the full penalty for our sins, He canceled forever every claim that the law of God had against us. It was as if He took all the divine ordinances that demanded our condemnation and nailed them to the cross (Colossians 2:14). "O the bliss of this glorious thought!"

The closing verse looks forward to the day when the Lord will consummate our redemption. Even our bodies will be redeemed, and everything good we have hoped for will be realized ("the faith shall be sight"—cf. Romans 8:22-25). In the meantime—and even while we're suffering unspeakable earthly grief—true believers in Christ can find sufficient comfort in knowing that all is eternally well with their souls.

FROM OUT OF THE PAST
Bobbie Wolgemuth

EVEN AS A YOUNG MAN Horatio G. Spafford was known as a man of refinement and unusual intelligence, an avid student of Scripture. His desire to be a man of God was reflected in his activities.

In the prime years of his financial success as a Chicago attorney, he knew that success at work needed to be balanced by success both at home and in the church. He loved his wife, four daughters, and son and was an active member of a Presbyterian church. He was also a loyal friend and supporter of D. L. Moody and other Christian leaders of the day. He continued to build a solid spiritual foundation as he built up his business ventures. The rock on which he built his faith would prove more valuable than any earthly possessions in the devastating crises he was to face in his early forties.

Spafford's only son died just months before his large real estate investment was wiped out in the Chicago Fire of 1871. Reeling from the family and financial loss, Spafford planned a trip to Europe for his family to coincide with an evangelistic crusade with Moody. At the last minute a business development delayed him, but as scheduled he sent his wife and four daughters ahead on the *S.S. Ville du Havre* to cross the Atlantic Ocean to Great Britain, where he was planning to join them a few days later.

The ship carrying his precious family was struck by an English vessel and sank in twelve minutes. All four of his daughters drowned. His wife survived the disaster and was taken to Wales, where she cabled her husband with the words, "Saved alone." Right away Spafford left by ship to join his wife. The captain of his vessel, knowing his deep bereavement, paused on his journey across the ocean to show Spafford the place where Bessie, Annie, Maggie, and Tanetta had drowned. It was there that the "sorrows like sea billows" rolled over his soul. Knowing that God "regarded my helpless estate," he penned the words that have brought deep comfort to generations of those facing unfathomable sorrows. The early years of Spafford's study of the character of God led him to the hope that someday his "faith shall be sight, the clouds be rolled back as a scroll" and thus he could confidently say, "It is well, it is well with my soul."

O Worship the King

ROBERT GRANT

1779-1838

O worship the King all-glorious above,
O gratefully sing his pow'r and his love;
our shield and Defender, the Ancient of Days,
pavilioned in splendor and girded with praise.

O tell of his might, O sing of his grace,
whose robe is the light, whose canopy space.
His chariots of wrath the deep thunderclouds form,
and dark is his path on the wings of the storm.

The earth with its store of wonders untold,
Almighty, your pow'r has founded of old;
has 'stablished it fast by a changeless decree,
and round it has cast, like a mantle, the sea.

Your bountiful care what tongue can recite?
It breathes in the air; it shines in the light;
it streams from the hills; it descends to the plain;
and sweetly distils in the dew and the rain.

Frail children of dust, and feeble as frail,
in you do we trust, nor find you to fail;
your mercies how tender, how firm to the end,
our Maker, Defender, Redeemer, and Friend!

O measureless Might! Ineffable Love!
While angels delight to hymn you above,
the humbler creation, though feeble their lays,
with true adoration shall lisp to your praise.

At the Heart of the Hymn

Robert Wolgemuth

❧

"S HE PROBABLY WON'T RECOGNIZE YOU," Dr. James Dobson said to Bobbie and me as he ushered us into his aging mother's hospital room. "Yesterday she didn't know who I was."

In a few minutes we were sitting on the edge of Myrtle Dobson's bed. Suffering from Parkinson's disease, which rendered her confused, she was unable to speak more than a word or two at a time. At first we didn't know if she recognized anyone in the room, but she was awake and seemed alert. Dr. Dobson spoke kindly to his mother, graciously reminding her who we were, even though we had known her very well. She nodded and smiled.

After a few minutes of small talk, Bobbie spoke up. "Why don't we sing. Myrtle loves to sing."

O worship the King all-glorious above,
O gratefully sing his pow'r and his love;
Our shield and Defender, the Ancient of Days,
Pavilioned in splendor and girded with praise.

For the first few lines of the hymn, she silently smiled back at us. Could she understand? Was she listening? We really couldn't tell.

As we sang a final verse, Myrtle's eyes began to sparkle. We knew she recognized this great hymn. Her mouth began first to form the words; then she joined in with each unforgettable word. What was even more amazing than Myrtle's remembering the lyrics to this great hymn was the fact that she sang a perfect alto. Many hymns followed, and she almost flawlessly recalled nearly every word.

The music may not have been strong enough to land a record contract, but it was good enough to fill our hearts with enough gratitude and praise to last a lifetime.

Frail children of dust, and feeble as frail,
In you do we trust, nor find you to fail;
Your mercies how tender, how firm to the end,
Our Maker, Defender, Redeemer, and Friend!

Dr. Dobson wept almost uncontrollably at the familiar sound of his mother singing this great melody of faith.

That afternoon we got a glimpse of the fullness of God's complete and perfect grace. This once vigorous woman, no longer having the capacity to even stand, was the picture of "frail children … and feeble as frail." But as the faithful wife of an artist, college professor, and traveling evangelist, her heart sang of God's trustworthiness. And as the mother of an active and gifted son, she knew of God's inability to fail.

Now, at the close of her life Myrtle Dobson was singing of God's tender mercy, good to the very end.

This hymn includes what may be the most powerful four-word summary of the character of the Sovereign God of the Universe ever recorded: "Maker, Defender, Redeemer, and Friend." Think of it! *Maker:* He created us. *Defender:* The forces of evil melt at the sound of His name. *Redeemer:* The death of His own Son was not too high a ransom to pay. *Friend:* A woman too weak to sit without help had Someone who reassured her of His everlasting presence.

As we drove away from the small hospital that Sunday afternoon, a light rain began to fall. For the first few minutes there was no talking, only the rhythmic sound of the windshield wipers. What we had experienced was too holy, too sanctified to discuss.

Almost two years later Myrtle Dobson went home to be with her Lord. Some of the well-wishers at the visitation reminded Dr. Dobson of his mother's great love of life and wonderful humor. Years before she had quipped that she thought her tombstone should read, "I told you I was sick!" They all laughed as they remembered.

But no one needed to be reminded that this precious woman had finished well. At an early age she had been introduced to the King as her personal Savior and had spent her life being filled with awe and worshiping Him. And now she could sing in His very presence in exquisite harmony.

IN THE LIGHT OF THE WORD
John MacArthur

THIS BELOVED HYMN WAS WRITTEN by Robert Grant but was based on a metered Psalm first published in 1561 by William Kethe. Kethe's work was a poetic adaptation of Psalm 104: "Praise the Lord, O my soul. O Lord my God, you are very great; you are clothed with splendor and majesty. He wraps himself in light as with a garment" (verses 1-2).

Here are the first three stanzas of Kethe's original work:

My soul, Praise the Lord, speak good of his Name,
O Lord our great God, how dost thou appear!
So passing in glory, that great is thy fame,
Honor and Majesty in thee shine most clear.

With light as a robe thou hast thyself clad,
Whereby all the earth thy greatness may see:
The heav'ns in such sort thou also hast spread,
That they to a curtain compared may be.

His chamber-beams lie in the clouds full sure,
Which as his chariots are made him to bear:
And there with much swiftness his course doth endure,
Upon the wings riding of winds in the air.

Grant's work is both fresh and original, but its pedigree is also evident. Grant borrowed expressions from Kethe, who drew his ideas from Psalm 104. The result is a wonderful hymn of pure praise based on allusions to that Psalm. Its theme is God's regal splendor and the inexpressible glory of His heavenly throne. He reigns "all-glorious above."

Biblical allusions run through the hymn, some of them going beyond Psalm 104. The expression "our shield and Defender" is a reference to Psalm 33:20 ("he is our help and our shield"). "Ancient of Days" is a name for God used only in Daniel 7, emphasizing His eternality and His sovereignty over time itself (see notes on "Immortal, Invisible, God Only Wise"). "Pavilioned in splendor" is a poetic way of saying that God dwells in a tabernacle of sheer, dazzling brilliance. "Girded with praise" suggests that He wears praise like a kingly garment. Such expressions are reminiscent of Psalm 22:3, which says, "But thou art holy, O thou that inhabitest the praises of Israel" (KJV). The praises of God's people thus become the garment in which He is enthroned, and that is how His glory is set on display through our worship.

The second stanza continues the call to worship: "O tell of His might, O sing of his grace." His might and His grace might seem to be virtually opposite attributes, and yet there is no conflict within God. His might and His grace are equally glorious and are perfectly in harmony.

The message of Psalm 104 comes through most clearly here in the second stanza. Every line in this stanza echoes the opening verses of that Psalm.

Stanza 4 rejoices in the "bountiful care" of the Lord toward His people. The imagery of this verse is beautiful, emphasizing that the Lord's tender mercy is everywhere evident in nature. "It breathes in the air" means that even the air God gives us to breathe is proof of His loving-kindness and care for us. "It shines in the light" suggests that daylight is another token of God's goodness. His bountiful care is evident even in the water that sustains earthly life. And here the hymn-writer has produced a sublime bit of poetry, picturing God's goodness like the water that "streams from the hills [and] descends to the plain; and sweetly distills in the dew and the rain." All of this is a superb paraphrase of Psalm 104:8-13.

The fifth stanza expresses our feeble frailness as "children of dust"—creatures formed from the dust of the earth. We know our own proneness to failure and defeat all too well. But the God in whom we trust has never been found to "fail."

This confession of frailty is significant when we realize that it came from the pen of a man who was the epitome of earthly prominence. Robert Grant's father was a member of the British Parliament, and he himself served for a time as governor of Bombay, India. Yet as a believer he fully recognized his own feeble susceptibility to human failure.

God still gives grace and tender mercy to the humble (1 Peter 5:5). There's a subtle paradox in the expression "your mercies how tender, how firm to the end." God's mercies are "tender" in one sense, "firm" in another. They are "tender" toward the needy sinner, yet "firm" in their steadfastness. They mirror the faithfulness of the One who is "Our Maker, Defender, Redeemer, and Friend."

From Out of the Past

Bobbie Wolgemuth

❧

ROBERT GRANT WAS EXPOSED to high political life from the time he was a small boy. He was born in Bengal, India, where his father was director of the East India Company and a respected member of the British Parliament, from Scotland. His family was careful to instill a love of the church and evangelistic pursuits in young Robert, which led him to involvement in missionary outreach throughout his life.

Coupled with Robert's pursuit of political life was a devout love for God. One year before he was appointed to the high position of Governor of Bombay, India, he wrote the hymn "O Worship the King." In spite of his own political pursuits, it was in his heart to position the Lord above all earthly power. Grant lets us peek at the glory of the true King in the highest place of honor, One who is eternally "pavilioned in splendor."

The strong description of God as "Ancient of Days" and our "Maker, Defender, Redeemer" leads us to adoration. To add that this powerful God is also our "Friend" is more than we can comprehend. Worship is our only response. The praises that surround the throne are ours.

The fifth verse of the hymn shows the compassionate heart of God and also of the hymn-writer. Robert calls the "feeble" and "frail" to trust in God whose "mercies" are "tender" and "firm to the end." This would have brought comfort to the sick and sorrowful he faithfully served. Robert Grant cared so deeply for the people of India that when he died at the age of fifty-nine, the ones he served expressed their strong love by establishing a medical college as a lasting memorial bearing his name.

Know Whom I Have Believed

DANIEL WEBSTER WHITTLE

1840-1901

I know not why God's wondrous grace to me he has made known,
nor why, unworthy, Christ in love redeemed me for his own.

CHORUS:
But "I know whom I have believed,
and am persuaded that he is able
to keep that which I've committed
unto him against that day."

I know not how this saving faith to me he did impart,
nor how believing in his Word wrought peace within my heart.

CHORUS

I know not how the Spirit moves, convincing men of sin,
revealing Jesus through the Word, creating faith in him.

CHORUS

I know not what of good or ill may be reserved for me,
of weary ways or golden days, before his face I see.

CHORUS

I know not when my Lord may come, at night or noonday fair,
nor if I'll walk the vale with him, or "meet him in the air,"

CHORUS

At the Heart of the Hymn

Robert Wolgemuth

༄

*T*HE MODESTLY APPOINTED GYMNASIUM-TURNED-SANCTUARY was filled with hundreds of people. The cumulative look on their faces was one of shock and disbelief. Many were softly weeping. What no one would have anticipated in even the wildest dreams had, in fact, come true. The lives of five men and one woman had been mysteriously snatched from the sky.

In spite of the fact that he personally represented some of the most publicly celebrated athletes and coaches in America, Robert Fraley was a private man. On October 25, 1999, Robert, his colleague Van Ardan, their friend Payne Stewart, and three others climbed aboard a private jet. Their expected touchdown two hours later was Love Field in downtown Dallas. But when the wheels of their airplane left the runway in Orlando, safely retracting into their appointed hollow, it would be the last time.

Because of the presence of the reigning U.S. Open Golf champion (Stewart) on board and the unfolding epic flight of a seemingly pilotless aircraft screaming through the October sky, Robert's privacy was about to be exploded around the world.

Within an hour of liftoff, news stations were interrupting their broadcasts with live reports. A private jet, possibly registered to Payne Stewart, seemed to be flying on its own. Air traffic controllers cleared the airspace by diverting commercial aircraft, so as not to interfere with the path of the unmanned airplane. Military jets were summoned to provide escort.

"The windows seem to be frosted from the inside," came the news from the sky. Experts were consulted as to why. Decompression of the cabin and estimates of temperatures of 70 degrees below zero seemed to be the most plausible scenario.

Three hours later the Learjet, having mercifully run out of fuel, plummeted to the ground in a remote portion of northeast South Dakota. Thousands of shards lay smoldering on the ground. Pictures of the scene were broadcast around the world.

Robert Fraley's family and friends gathered to say good-bye to their friend. Eulogies and words of comfort from Holy Scripture were delivered with dignity and passion, worthy of this gifted, sober, and godly man.

As the service drew to a close, the piano player began the opening strains of the simple melody to "I Know Whom I Have Believed." A radiant, young woman stood at a single microphone, and with a voice as clear and strong as the character of this precious friend she sang each verse and the powerful refrain.

> But "I know whom I have believed,
> And am persuaded that he is able
> To keep that which I've committed
> Unto him against that day."

As she sang the last verse, it almost felt as if the songwriter had had a divine premonition.

> I know not when my Lord may come,
> At night or noonday fair,
> Nor if I'll walk the vale with him,
> Or "meet him in the air."

Audible gasps came from many. Others were stunned with the ominous impact of the moment. Our friend, Robert, his three colleagues, and two pilots—all believers—had been taken safely home from midair.

What they thought was a routine flight from Central Florida to Central Texas had become a resplendent one-way excursion to Glory.

IN THE LIGHT OF THE WORD

John MacArthur

⟨◦⟩

*T*HE CHORUS OF THIS BELOVED GOSPEL SONG is taken verbatim from the *King James Version's* wording of the final phrase in 2 Timothy 1:12: "I know whom I have believed, and am persuaded that he is able to keep that which I have committed unto him against that day." It is as thoroughly biblical as any hymn could ever be.

Songwriter Daniel W. Whittle simply borrowed Paul's words to Timothy and made them his own testimony in this chorus about the absolute certainty of the true believer's unshakable security in Christ. The song, first published in 1887, has been a popular favorite for more than a century.

Whittle was a Chicago businessman and a close friend of evangelist D. L. Moody. In 1873 Whittle left his job as treasurer for the Elgin Watch Company to become a full-time evangelist himself.

Like his famous mentor, Whittle lacked formal theological training. But he also shared Mr. Moody's love for the Word of God, and his mind and heart were brimming with Scripture. (This is evident in all his best-loved gospel songs, including "The Church of God Is One," "Christ Liveth in Me," and "There Shall Be Showers of Blessing.") In fact, Whittle's familiarity with the Bible and his commitment to the authority of Scripture kept him refreshingly sound in an era when the nation's most influential seminaries were aggressively indoctrinating students with modernism and other rationalistic, humanistic philosophies. Such trends were laying a foundation for theological liberalism in the early twentieth century.

Meanwhile, "I Know Whom I Have Believed" became something of an evangelical battle-hymn against the skepticism promoted by that kind of religious liberalism.

Whittle juxtaposes the triumphantly confident words of 2 Timothy 1:12 against several statements about what the believer cannot know. Each stanza begins with the words "I know not," making the words of the chorus even more emphatic: "But 'I know . . .'"

The song therefore acknowledges and extols the many mysteries of the Christian faith even as it unequivocally affirms the utter certainty upon which the Gospel is based. Notice what the song cites as truths that are hidden from us:

The mystery of divine grace and God's election: The first stanza is an expression of wonder at the fact that God has sovereignly chosen and redeemed those who, by their own confession, have no rightful claim to His grace. "I know not why God's wondrous grace to me He has made known." We do not know why God bestows His grace on us; it certainly cannot be because of anything worthy He sees (or foresees) in us.

The mystery of saving faith: The second stanza acknowledges that even our faith is a gift from God. "I know not how this saving faith to me He did impart." How He imparts faith to us is as mysterious as why He chose us. As is true of so many great Christian hymns and gospel songs, these words grow out of the essential conviction that God is sovereign in the salvation of sinners. Every aspect of our salvation—including our faith—is God's work, not our own. He imparts faith; true faith is not something conjured up by human willpower.

The mystery of regeneration: Perhaps there's a deliberate allusion to John 3 in the third stanza—"I know not how the Spirit moves, convincing men of sin." Jesus told Nicodemus that the Holy Spirit is like the wind—invisible in the how and where of His work but obvious in the effects of it (John 3:8). Again this affirms God's sovereignty in salvation.

The mystery of Christ's return: The details of the return of Christ are also deliberately obscured from us (Mark 13:32). We cannot know precisely when He will come (Luke 12:40). And we cannot know ahead of time whether we will be taken into the Lord's presence by our death ("walk the vale with him") or by His coming ("meet him in the air").

These are all great mysteries—truths at least partially obscured from us. But these and other mysteries of the Christian faith do not diminish the rock-solid faithfulness of Christ or our certainty that He is able to keep what we have committed to Him.

From Out of the Past
Bobbie Wolgemuth

DANIEL WEBSTER WHITTLE WAS NO STRANGER to war and death. A Civil War veteran, Whittle accompanied Union general William Sherman on his march through Georgia and was wounded in the Battle of Vicksburg. Surrounded by fallen comrades and needing to know the reassuring power of God, his prayer could have been, "I write these things to you who believe in the name of the Son of God so that you may know that you have eternal life" (1 John 5:13).

Young Daniel's commitment to Christ came as a result of his mother's faithful prayers for him. Before he marched off to join the Illinois Infantry, barely out of his teen years, his mother tucked a small Bible into his backpack. When he became a prisoner of war, he read and reread those pages until personal belief in God and His Word "wrought peace within his heart." Daniel would later write, "I know not how the Spirit moves ... creating faith in him," describing the mystery of God's incredible grace.

At the end of the war, Major Whittle returned to Chicago, where he became treasurer of the Elgin Watch Company. Surrounded now by clocks and time-pieces, he pondered the timeless eternity of his faithful God. After a short time, not knowing when his own life would wind to an end, he was persuaded by D. L. Moody to spend his remaining years as an evangelist and hymn-writer. This Civil War veteran, POW, and successful businessman penned over 200 hymn texts before his death at age sixty-one, including "There Shall be Showers of Blessing," "The Banner of the Cross," and "Christ Liveth in Me." The verse from his mother's Bible that inspired this much-loved hymn was 2 Timothy 1:12. Like a major confidently assuring his officers, the Apostle Paul writes to young Timothy, "I know whom I have believed, and am persuaded that he is able to keep that which I have committed unto him against that day."

O the Deep, Deep Love of Jesus

SAMUEL TREVOR FRANCIS
1834-1925

O the deep, deep love of Jesus! Vast, unmeasured, boundless free;
rolling as a mighty ocean in its fullness over me.
Underneath me, all around me, is the current of thy love;
Leading onward, leading homeward, to thy glorious rest above.

O the deep, deep love of Jesus! Spread his praise from shore to shore;
how he loveth, ever loveth, changeth never, nevermore;
how he watches o'er his loved ones, died to call them all his own;
how for them he intercedeth, watcheth o'er them from the throne.

O the deep, deep love of Jesus! Love of ev'ry love the best:
'Tis an ocean vast of blessing, 'tis a haven sweet of rest.
O the deep, deep love of Jesus! 'Tis a heav'n of heav'ns to me;
and it lifts me up to glory, for it lifts me up to thee.

AT THE HEART OF THE HYMN
Robert Wolgemuth

ఌ

"I LOVE YOU."

What three words have had more impact on our world than these? But who can adequately define what they really mean?

This is love: not that we loved God, but that he loved us and
sent his Son as an atoning sacrifice for our sins.

—1 JOHN 4:10

God's LOVE IS NOT FRAMED with words, but a Person. God's love is Jesus. In the summer of 1968 I got my first look at the Grand Canyon. I had seen photographs in my school library's encyclopedia. I had even received a postcard from a vacationing friend, picturing the expanse. But I was not prepared for the experience of standing on the rim of this gargantuan chasm. The best way to describe this spectacular scene is to say that it's completely indescribable.

A century ago a songwriter stepped to the precipice of God's limitless love and wrote the words to this hymn. Samuel Trevor Francis had never seen the Grand Canyon, but he surely knew the emotion.

O the deep, deep love of Jesus!
Vast, unmeasured, boundless, free;
Rolling as a mighty ocean
In its fullness over me.

Can you see him, groping for words to illustrate God's love in Jesus? Can you hear the desperate attempt to put words to the indescribable? Can you feel the heart of a man who had experienced God's love to the core of his soul? I can too.

Several years ago as I was pulling out of the parking lot where I often rented power tools, I spotted a child. Directly across the street from the rental store was a day-care center. A six-foot chain-link fence surrounded the playground. Lots of children were busily playing on the swing sets, sandboxes, and jungle gyms scattered throughout the area. Several supervisors were wandering around. But what caught my eye was a little girl no more than three years old. She was wearing a light blue jumper and was standing by herself. Tears were streaming down her face. No one was playing with her. No one was talking to her. She was just standing there, looking very sad.

I had just returned a chainsaw and was headed home for a shower. My day had been filled with hard, filthy work, and I was ready for some rest. But I sat there in my pickup, gazing at the little girl in the corner of the playground. Soon my own eyes were brimming with tears.

More than anything I wanted to park my truck, run across the street, jump the fence, and wrap my arms around her. I wanted to hold the little girl until she stopped crying. I wanted to tell her that even though I'm a busy, fast-moving grown-up, sometimes I know exactly what it feels like to be a little kid softly weeping in the corner of the playground. And I wanted to reassure her that someone who loved her would surely come to get her soon.

I sat there in my truck and silently asked Jesus to surround her with His love. To comfort her and fill her with Himself. And I thanked Him for the times when His love and presence have been enough for me—when all I needed was to feel the indescribable arms of my heavenly Father and know more of His deep, deep love.

And it lifts me up to glory,
For it lifts me up to thee.

I drove out of the rental parking lot and headed home. Determined to look carefully for ways to bring more tenderness to my own family and friends, I was grateful for the little girl in the corner of the playground and for Jesus' unfathomable love.

IN THE LIGHT OF THE WORD

John MacArthur

D IVINE LOVE IS A COMMON THEME in our hymnology, but aside from the inspired Psalms, no hymn expresses the profundity of Jesus' love any better than this one. Words and music function perfectly together to heighten the sense of the infinite greatness of our Savior's redeeming love, which is "vast, unmeasured, boundless, free."

The first stanza speaks of the infinite scope and boundlessness of divine love, bringing to mind the words of the apostle Paul, who spoke of "how wide and long and high and deep is the love of Christ" (Ephesians 3:18). By reason of its sheer vastness, this rolling ocean of love might seem enormous in an impersonal sense. But the hymn-writer stresses the individual intimacy of Christ's love as it flows "over me, underneath me, all around me."

The imagery is perfect. The believer, totally immersed in Christ's love, is swept along by its current as it carries him heavenward. Like ocean water, the love completely envelops him, leaving no aspect of his person untouched. He is soaked in it. It is a comforting and refreshing ablution, making us fit for heaven while taking us there, to our "glorious rest above."

The second stanza celebrates the perpetual constancy of Christ's love. Since Christ is completely unchanging ("Jesus Christ is the same yesterday and today and forever," Hebrews 13:8), His love is immutable as well: "He loveth, ever loveth." John 13:1 says of Jesus' love for His disciples: "Having loved his own who were in the world, he now showed them the full extent of his love." The Greek text uses an expression that could be translated "loved them to the uttermost." Thus Scripture stresses both the steadfastness and the supreme excellence of Christ's love for His own.

The hymn then points out the redemptive proofs of Christ's love toward His people: "How he watches o'er his loved ones, Died to call them all his own." Jesus Himself said, "This is the will of him who sent me, that I should lose none of all that he has given me, but raise them up at the last day" (John 6:39). The expression "all that he has given me" refers to people—the elect—promised to Him and given to Him by the Father, but in need of redemption from their own sin at the price of Christ's blood. They are therefore a mutual love-gift—promised by the Father to the Son, but purchased by the Son for the Father through His loving submission to the Father's will. And in turn, both Father and Son love them with an infinite, inviolable love.

Christ's love is therefore a protective love. On the night of His betrayal He prayed, "While I was with them, I protected them and kept them safe by that name you gave me. None has been lost …" (John 17:12). Now in heaven, "he intercedeth, watcheth o'er them from the throne!" His prayers for us from heaven echo His High Priestly prayer in John 17. He prays for our protection from evil. He prays for our perseverance in the faith. "Therefore he is able to save completely those who come to God through him, because he always lives to intercede for them" (Hebrews 7:25).

The third stanza recaps the hymn-writer's wonder at the vastness and superiority of Christ's love, "Love of every love the best." He regards the love of Christ as both a vast ocean and a peaceful haven of rest. He testifies that Christ's love is "a heav'n of heav'ns"—a blessed foretaste of heaven, enabling us to experience something of the true heavenly glory even here in this life through the love of Christ, which, in the hymn-writer's words, "lifts me up to Thee."

FROM OUT OF THE PAST

Bobbie Wolgemuth

*T*HE RENEWED INTEREST in congregational singing had a great influence on the churches in England in the nineteenth and early twentieth centuries. When parishioners were given understandable, inspirational, and doctrinally sound hymn texts, they experienced a renewed vitality in their response to God's grace.

Samuel Trevor Francis was a gifted devotional speaker in the Plymouth Brethren assemblies in Great Britain. Typically the home meetings of the congregation were unstructured, counting on "brothers" to minister as they were able. This was the call of Samuel Trevor Francis. Believing that "a spiritual church is a singing church," there was singing involved in every gathering. And this singing was done with no instrumental accompaniment—only the voices of those who met. There were various services throughout the week, including the Breaking of Bread, Reading Meetings, and assemblies that were clearly for evangelistic witness.

The purpose of worship was to address some dimension of the person and work of Jesus Christ. Often a theme would develop. What better theme for Samuel to approach than the deep love of God in His Incarnate Son?

The purpose of the hymn singing was to give the worshipers a clear picture of their position in Christ—His love, His salvation, and their need for holiness and obedience. The original text to "O the Deep, Deep Love of Jesus" gave a beautiful word picture of the all-encompassing love of the Savior. The rolling tones of the minor key to which it was set provided an introspective and unforgettable experience of worship. With the hearts of the people full, the comments of the sermon could be most effective.

Is it any wonder that Samuel Trevor Francis was known throughout Great Britain as an effective communicator? His hymn text wonderfully opened the door to the Holy Spirit before he spoke a word.

Man of Sorrows! What a Name

PHILIP P. BLISS
1838-1876

Man of Sorrows! what a name
for the Son of God, who came
ruined sinners to reclaim:
Hallelujah! what a Savior!

Bearing shame and scoffing rude,
in my place condemned he stood,
sealed my pardon with his blood:
Hallelujah! what a Savior!

Guilty, vile, and helpless, we;
spotless Lamb of God was he;
full atonement! can it be?
Hallelujah! what a Savior!

Lifted up was he to die,
"It is finished!" was his cry;
now in heav'n exalted high:
Hallelujah! what a Savior!

When he comes, our glorious King,
all his ransomed home to bring,
then anew this song we'll sing:
Hallelujah! what a Savior!

AT THE HEART OF THE HYMN

Joni Eareckson Tada

∾

He was despised and rejected by men,
a man of sorrows, and familiar with suffering.

—ISAIAH 53:3

A FRIGHTENED SEVENTEEN-YEAR-OLD GIRL lies faceup in a shadowy hospital room wondering if God has abandoned her to this strange, terrifying life of paralysis. The hallways are dark, and visiting hours are over, yet the girl turns her head on the pillow to discover a visitor. It's her high school girlfriend, Jacque, standing at the guardrail. "What are you doing here? If they catch you, they'll kick you out."

"Shh." The one standing motions, then lowers the guardrail to gingerly climb in alongside her friend, as though the two of them are at a girls' pajama party.

This, however, is no high school sleepover. This is a tragedy, and nothing—absolutely nothing—has been able to dispel the horror of a neck broken and a life destroyed. Until now the visitor has only shared milkshakes, hockey sticks, and boyfriends with the paralyzed girl. But Jacque instinctively knows the only thing that will comfort. In the darkness she sings softly:

Man of Sorrows! what a name
For the Son of God, who came
Ruined sinners to reclaim:
Hallelujah! what a Savior!

It's the best thing anyone could have done for that paralyzed girl. Lying long hours in bed, she had recited lots of verses about God's purposes in suffering, but that hadn't helped. Answers and reasons, good as they are, were not reaching the place where it hurt—in the gut and heart. The paralyzed teen was like a brokenhearted child looking up into the face of her daddy, asking, "Why?" She wasn't looking for answers so much as a daddy who would pick her up and tell her everything would be okay. Her unspoken plea was for assurance—fatherly assurance—that her world was not splitting apart at the seams.

That's what we all want when we're hurting. We want our Father to embrace us and give us Himself. And He does. In Psalm 18 He is our Rock and Deliverer. In Psalm 10 He becomes the Father to the orphaned. In Isaiah 9 He is the Wonderful Counselor to the confused and depressed. If you are the one at the center of the universe, holding it together so it doesn't split apart at the seams, if everything moves, breathes, and has its being in you, as it says of God in Acts 17:28, you can do no more than give yourself.

That was what Jacque helped her friend understand that night. God doesn't give those who hurt mere words. He gives the Word—Jesus, the bruised and bloody Man of Sorrows who endured hell on earth so that you and I, by trusting in Him, can escape it.

Last year I received an invitation to go back home for my thirtieth high school class reunion. I telephoned the chairman of the committee to make reservations and ask who else would be coming. There was a long pause when I asked about my hockey friends. "Joni, you probably didn't hear the news that was on television here last night. Jacque's teenage boy Josh had really been struggling and … well, he's dead … he committed suicide." There was another long silence. I hung up the phone in shock.

I tried to call Jacque but couldn't get through. I had to do something, so I wrote a letter:

Dear Jacque:

Ken and I are planning to be home for the reunion and I'm hoping we can see each other. If so, I would want to hold your hand, as you once held mine in the hospital, and I would softly sing to you, as you once sang to me, "Man of Sorrows! what a name . . ." I don't know what else to say. May the Man of Sorrows be your comfort. And, as in the hospital, I would hope you would sense what I felt and what I still remember to this day. Peace. Not answers, but peace. Do you remember that night more than 30 years ago? I have never forgotten it.

Love,

Joni

Weeks later Ken and I sat across a private dinner table from Jacque. Although her eyes were sad, thirty years and a few wrinkles, divorce, and the death of her son had not diminished the winsome, youthful optimism in her smile. When I asked how she was doing, she grew serious. She pressed her thumb and forefinger against a cross that hung around her neck and said quietly, "I hate what has happened. I can't talk to God. I can't pray. I'm angry, but I still need my connection to Him."

I watched the way she held the cross around her neck. The cross where God explained not with answers but with Himself. To this day, Jacque is discovering all that means. Just like her paralyzed friend.

In the Light of the Word

John MacArthur

ℰ

IT'S ONE OF THE GREAT IRONIES of all eternity that Christ, creator and sustainer of all things, was spurned in His incarnation by His own creatures and put to death by those to whom He gave life. It's ironic, too, that as He went to the cross in the supreme display of divine mercy toward humanity, the Son of Man Himself was "despised and rejected of men, a man of sorrows" (Isaiah 53:3). This marvelous song is a meditation on that irony and an expression of heartfelt praise to Christ for having willingly borne so much on behalf of sinners.

The words of the song are straightforward and clear. It is a poetic overview of the cross and a survey of the sufferings Christ bore there in the place of "ruined sinners" whom He would redeem through His sacrifice. Each verse ends in the same simple but profound outpouring of praise to Christ: "Hallelujah! what a Savior!"

Verse 1 evokes the context of Isaiah 53, the premiere Old Testament prophecy about the cross and the substitutionary work Christ did there. This stanza thus subtly reminds us that the sorrows Christ bore from Gethsemane to Calvary were foretold ages before His coming—proof that He subjected Himself to the cross and the hostile crowds willingly and deliberately, not out of weakness or helplessness.

The second verse speaks of the scorn that was heaped on Him by those who put Him to death. Scripture tells us He was brutally mocked and repeatedly taunted—both while on trial for His life and while He hung on the cross (Luke 22:64-65; Mark 15:29-32). The song reminds us that He took all that abuse because He stood condemned in our place. He was suffering what we rightfully deserve.

"His blood" thus "sealed my pardon." The imagery there is of a legal document scrolled up and sealed with an official seal to guarantee its legitimacy and legal efficacy. In this case the seal is written in blood—the blood of Christ Himself, who poured out His life with the express purpose of making pardon from sin possible.

The third verse continues in that same vein, reminding us that we, not He, deserved the pain and suffering and sorrows He bore. We are "guilty, vile and helpless." We are thoroughly corrupted by sin and unable to do anything to atone for our sins or make ourselves holy (Romans 3:10-12; 5:6). He, on the other hand, is the "Spotless Lamb of God." He is "holy, blameless, pure, set apart from sinners" (Hebrews 7:26). He "committed no sin, and no deceit was found in his mouth" (1 Peter 2:22).

Christ's spotless perfection was necessary for Him to render "full atonement." "It is impossible for the blood of bulls and of goats to take away sins" (Hebrews 10:4). Only "the blood of Christ, who through the eternal Spirit offered himself unblemished to God" (9:14) can accomplish that.

The fourth verse celebrates the once-for-all sufficiency of Christ's atoning death. "'It is finished!' was His cry." That refers to our Lord's dying words, recorded in John 19:30. With that final declaration He signified the utter completion of His redemptive work. He has done everything necessary to atone for the sins of believers. There is nothing they can do to supplement His work, nothing they may do to amplify or extend it. He has completed the perfect work of redemption entirely on their behalf.

Now He is in heaven and is exalted above all things (Philippians 2:9), showing that God was pleased with His work. Redemption for those who trust Christ is as certain as the Father's love for His Son.

The closing verse looks forward to the time when Christ will return for His people. Then we will sing "a new song" (Revelation 14:3), but it turns out to be precisely the same theme of praise to Christ that the church has sung from the beginning: "Hallelujah! what a Savior!"

FROM OUT OF THE PAST
Bobbie Wolgemuth

PHILIP BLISS WAS BORN into a Pennsylvania farm family too poor to offer him any formal musical training. When he was only twelve years old, he confessed his sins, received God's gift of grace, and joined a church near the lumber camps where he worked. He had an unusual talent for singing and especially loved the gospel music at church services. Through diligent study on his own, he became a proficient musician, music teacher, and one of the great hymnwriters of the nineteenth century. He would listen to sermons and meditate on the ideas until, often in one sitting, he would complete a song text and melody.

When Philip was twenty-six, he sold his first song to a Chicago publisher, who sent him a flute in exchange for the manuscript. He moved to Chicago to work for that publishing company, and there he met Dwight L. Moody. With his beautiful baritone voice, Philip was a natural addition to Moody's evangelistic services. Moody told the impressionable young man, "Singing does at least as much as preaching to impress the Word of God upon people's minds."

Bliss continued to put profound biblical truths into unadorned verse, then set the words to memorable music. He wrote, "O How I Love Jesus" so children could sing of God's great love. A collection of his music used by Sunday school teachers and evangelists entitled "Gospel Songs" gave rise to the gospel song movement across the nation. Adults as well as children enjoyed the new, refreshing style of sacred music.

Philip entered full-time evangelistic work, traveling with Major Daniel Whittle and Dwight Moody, and continued writing many familiar hymns, such as "Wonderful Words of Life," "I Gave My Life for Thee," "Almost Persuaded," and "Let the Lower Lights Be Burning."

Tragically, when Bliss was only thirty-eight years old he and his wife perished when traveling home from Christmas holidays in Pennsylvania. Their train overturned and fell into a deep ravine, killing the Blisses and 100 other passengers. The legacy of the brief thirty-eight years of Philip Bliss's life, however, steadfastly remains in his many hymns.

O Sacred Head, Now Wounded

BERNARD OF CLAIRVAUX
1091-1153

O sacred Head, now wounded, with grief and shame weighed down;
now scornfully surrounded with thorns, thine only crown;
O sacred Head, what glory, what bliss till now was thine!
Yet, though despised and gory, I joy to call thee mine.

What thou, my Lord, has suffered was all for sinners' gain:
mine, mine was the transgression, but thine the deadly pain.
Lo, here I fall, my Savior! 'Tis I deserve thy place;
look on me with thy favor, vouchsafe to me thy grace.

What language shall I borrow to thank thee, dearest Friend,
for this, thy dying sorrow, thy pity without end?
O make me thine forever; and should I fainting be,
Lord, let me never, never outlive my love to thee.

At the Heart of the Hymn

Joni Eareckson Tada

᠊᠊᠊

They put a purple robe on him, then twisted together a crown of thorns and set it on him. And they began to call out to him, "Hail, king of the Jews!" Again and again they struck him on the head with a staff and spit on him. Falling on their knees, they paid homage to him. And when they had mocked him, they took off the purple robe and put his own clothes on him. Then they led him out to crucify him.

—MARK 15:17-20

"O HAPPY DAY, O-o-o happy day …" the worship leader boomed into the microphone, clapping and swaying and stirring smiles among the congregation. Mothers bounced their babies on their knees, and a few waved their bulletins in time with the music. It was Good Friday and, being far away from home, I was visiting a friend's church. Although the mood was cheery and the songs were festive, I was glad to be sitting in the back row. It didn't feel like Good Friday.

I was raised in a little Reformed Episcopal Church that took Good Friday seriously. The service was somber, the hymns were sober, and sometimes a black cloth was draped over the Communion table. Once, to represent each year of Jesus' earthly life, the bell in the tower tolled thirty-three times—slowly, so that each strike of the hammer on metal resonated through the sanctuary, like someone driving a spike. As each gong echoed, the choir dispersed, some walking down the center aisle, some along the side, and others down the back of the choir loft. They looked like disciples abandoning their Lord, scattering and not looking back.

No one dismissed the congregation. A few people in the pews looked around nervously, not knowing exactly what to do. Some got up and left. Others, like me, sat and let the moment sink in. This is what it was like the night they took Jesus away, I thought. Nobody knew what to do then either. Hot tears filled my eyes as the hymn we had sung earlier, "O Sacred Head, Now Wounded," hit me:

Mine, mine was the transgression,
But thine the deadly pain.
Lo, here I fall, my Savior!
'Tis I deserve thy place.

There was no casual chatter in the narthex. No organ postlude. Just silence and footsteps. Only in the parking lot did life get back to normal.

As a child, the seriousness of Mark 15:17-20 was branded into my memory. I learned early on that although Jesus' being crucified on my behalf is cause for celebration, first I need to appreciate the enormous weight of such a sacrifice.

That's why my heart ached as I sat in the back row of my friend's church. Maybe I'm old-fashioned; perhaps I'm placing too much on childhood memories and not moving ahead with the times. More to the point, some would agree with my friend who, after church ended, said, "Joni, why do you want to be somber on a night like this? Jesus didn't stay on the cross—He arose. That fact alone changes everything."

On the books, she's right.

Still, we have a month of Sundays to sing happy Scripture choruses and bright, rousing hymns. We have only one day set aside in the entire church calendar to ponder the gravity of Jesus' wounds. Is that asking too much? I smiled at my friend as she motioned me on to the potluck in the next hall.

I sighed and followed, humming, "O Sacred Head."

In the Light of the Word
John MacArthur

⁓

THIS IS A VERY EARLY HYMN, dating back to the twelfth century. Bernard of Clairvaux's words were translated into German and set to a chorale tune during the Reformation. It became a staple in the Lutheran churches, and in the early 1700s Johann Sebastian Bach made the familiar chorale a centerpiece in his famous oratorio *The Passion According to St. Matthew.*

It is a poignant hymn of worship with the dying Savior in view. Most modern hymnbooks give abbreviated versions; the original Lutheran version of the hymn had at least ten stanzas, each focusing on a different aspect of Christ's sufferings and the believer's response to the cross.

The first stanza focuses on the painful and humiliating crown of thorns. What an awful irony that Christ set aside His heavenly throne and glory for this ("O sacred Head, what glory, what bliss till now was thine!")! He deserved the most glorious heavenly crown; He received instead a cruel, mocking crown of thorns.

The effects of Christ's sufferings left that sacred Head badly disfigured, swollen, bruised, and bleeding. Isaiah prophetically described the scene at the cross in these graphic terms: "He had no beauty or majesty to attract us to him, nothing in his appearance that we should desire him. He was despised and rejected by men, a man of sorrows, and familiar with suffering. Like one from whom men hide their faces he was despised, and we esteemed him not" (Isaiah 53:2-3).

But the believer, looking back on the cross with gratitude, can say with the hymn-writer, "Yet, though despised and gory, I joy to call thee mine."

One of the original stanzas missing from most modern hymnbooks adds these details about what our redemption cost the Savior:

Men mock and taunt and jeer thee,
Thou noble countenance,
Though mighty worlds shall fear thee
And flee before thy glance.

It is unfathomable that the Lord of glory would condescend to accept such abuse from sinful men, especially considering the fact that one day every creature will kneel before Him and acknowledge His rightful lordship. He could have utterly destroyed his oppressors on the spot with a single word, but He was on a mission of mercy and redemption. "For God sent not his Son into the world to condemn the world, but to save the world through him" (John 3:17).

The hymn-writer vividly describes the physical effects of the cross on the Savior:

How art thou pale with anguish,
With sore abuse and scorn!
How does that visage languish
Which once was bright as morn!

Our middle stanza gives the meaning of Christ's suffering on the cross. His sufferings were "all for sinners' gain." We committed the transgressions; but He bore all the suffering and anguish that resulted from our sin, even though He had no guilt of His own. He did this by putting Himself in the place of His people, bearing the full brunt of divine wrath and the penalty of divine justice on their behalf.

The only appropriate response for us as believers is to fall on our faces in humble gratitude, acknowledging that we, not He, deserved such suffering and anguish. ("'tis I deserve thy place.") We must also plead for even more of the grace and tender mercy that prompted Him to die for us. ("Look on me with thy favor, vouchsafe to me thy grace.")

The final verse is an expression of profound thankfulness to Christ for His sacrifice. Human language is totally insufficient to express the gratitude the true believer owes Christ. "What language shall I borrow to thank thee?" The only appropriate response is the surrender of one's whole life and self to the Lord.

I especially love the final prayer of the hymn, which basically expresses a preference for being put to death rather than allowing one's love for Christ to diminish.

From Out of the Past

Bobbie Wolgemuth

*T*HE TIME IN HISTORY known as "the Dark Ages" was not without people who displayed God's radiant light. The institution of the church during this time was characterized by corruption and disgrace, but into this darkness was born Bernard of Clairvaux, who at a tender age showed interest in scholarship and spiritual piety.

His father was a knight, and his mother was known for her gentle goodness. Bernard announced in his early twenties that he had chosen to be a monk, laying aside his opportunities to achieve nobility and lead a prosperous temporal life. His decision proved to bring out the best of his leadership qualities and dynamic personality and talents. The ministry that emerged from Bernard's call became one of the most influential throughout all of Europe. His platform gave him the

ability to hold sway over kings, emperors, and the multitudes to whom he elo-
quently preached. It was said that crowds of vicious men had conversion expe-
riences due to his strong and confrontational challenge to repent and exercise
personal faith. Many of these converts unashamedly carried crosses as symbols of
their commitment to Christ.

Besides writing many books on church-related issues, Bernard was an accomplished poet. His work included the lyrics of such hymns as "Jesus, the Very
Thought of Thee" and "Jesus, Thou Joy of Loving Hearts." One of his poems
focused on the heart, knees, feet, hands, side, breast, and finally the face of Jesus
as he suffered on the cross. Bernard's description of Jesus' face was translated from
Latin into German by a hymn-writer who had suffered the loss of his young
wife and all four of his children. This poem became the words to the hymn "O
Sacred Head, Now Wounded."

Bernard's love of the Savior was so evident that Martin Luther wrote that
Bernard "was the best monk who ever lived" and that "Bernard loved Jesus as
much as anyone could." His dedication to a life of simplicity, discipline, and
prayer and his personal love for Jesus motivated Bernard of Clairvaux to found
162 monasteries during his lifetime and to pen some of the most endearing words
that draw us to reflect on the person and passion of Jesus.

Immortal, Invisible, God Only Wise

WALTER CHALMERS SMITH

1824-1908

Immortal, invisible, God only wise,
in light inaccessible hid from our eyes,
most blessed, most glorious, the Ancient of Days,
almighty, victorious, thy great name we praise.

Unresting, unhasting and silent as light,
nor wanting, nor wasting, thou rulest in might;
thy justice like mountains high soaring above
thy clouds which are fountains of goodness and love.

Great Father of glory, pure Father of light,
thine angels adore thee, all veiling their sight;
all praise we would render; O help us to see
'tis only the splendor of light hideth thee!

AT THE HEART OF THE HYMN

Joni Eareckson Tada

꘎

*After consulting the people, Jehoshaphat appointed men to sing to the Lord and
to praise him for the splendor of his holiness as they went out at the head of the
army, saying, "Give thanks to the Lord, for his love endures forever." As they
began to sing and praise, the Lord set ambushes against the men of Ammon
and Moab and Mount Seir who were invading Judah, and they were defeated.*

—2 CHRONICLES 20:21-22

REMEMBER THAT DARK PATH you once walked on a windy night
under a full moon? The trees hunched down, their branches scraping and groping like fingers of a phantom. An owl screeched. Leaves swirled. A cloud eclipsed
the moon, darkening your path. Remember what you did? (Okay, so it was a
dark parking lot and it wasn't moonlight but streetlight, not an owl but a police
siren. The point is, you've been there, right?) So, what did you do?

You sang. Or at least whistled.

It's a common reaction for a good reason. Since the days of Jehoshaphat, people facing fear have resorted to song. But for God's people, it's not just any old
song that chases away dark spirits. When Jehoshaphat was confronted by a huge
military machine of Ammonites and Moabites, he had his people fast and pray,
and then he assembled his troops. But who comprised his front line? The cavalry?
The infantry? No; it was a choir. These singers had orders to do much more
than whistle in the dark; they were to march out before the Israelite army and
praise the beauty of God's holiness. And when they began to sing and to praise,
the opposition was thrown into confusion. Befuddled, their camps turned on

one another. Jehoshaphat's army then made a shambles of the enemy, carrying away the plunder.

This is good news for any Christian who's afraid of the dark because songs of praise clear the spiritual air like nothing else. If you're in the middle of spiritual conflict, if the enemy is poised and ready to attack, the best defense is to sing. It's a way of resisting the devil. Singing is also the best offense. Songs of praise will confuse the enemy and send the devil's hordes hightailing.

And if you're looking for a hymn that praises the beauty of God's attributes, there's no better hymn to sing when you are under attack (or afraid of the dark) than …

Immortal, invisible, God only wise,
In light inaccessible hid from our eyes,
Most blessed, most glorious, the Ancient of Days,
Almighty, victorious, thy great name we praise.

The words to "Immortal, Invisible, God Only Wise" are a doxology of song, each stanza turning up the wattage on God's glory. This hymn shines like a flashlight—no, a searchlight—that dispels the darkness. As we sing and proclaim our "Great Father of glory, pure Father of light," our path is illuminated, and the true identity of the shadowy forms of things around us is revealed. This beautiful old hymn extols the exalted attributes of God—His justice, goodness, mercy, and love—and is like a flamethrower, incinerating every discouraging thought and every anxiety and fear. When we sing "Immortal, Invisible, God Only Wise" we find ourselves on the front lines, advancing against the enemy. The devil's armies have no choice but to retreat.

Amy Carmichael, missionary to India, wrote, "I truly believe that Satan cannot endure the power of song and so slips out of the room—more or less—when there is a hymn of praise. Prayer rises more easily, more spontaneously, after one has let those wings, words and music carry one out of oneself into that upper air."

Victory over the enemy can be yours for a song.

In the Light of the Word
John MacArthur

THIS CLASSIC HYMN OF PURE PRAISE, set to a traditional Welsh melody, is one of the most polished works of poetry in the hymnbook. It is also a thoroughly biblical exposition of the chief attributes of God.

The opening line paraphrases the apostle Paul's opening benediction in 1 Timothy 1:17:

> *Now to the King eternal, immortal, invisible, the only God, be honor and*
> *glory for ever and ever. Amen.*

Paul closed 1 Timothy with a similar paean to God:

> *Who alone is immortal and who lives in unapproachable light, whom no one*
> *has seen or can see. To him be honor and might forever. Amen." (6:16)*

The second line of this hymn is drawn from that verse.

God is "eternal" because He always preexisted and will forever endure—without beginning and without end. He is both Alpha and Omega, Beginning and End (Revelation 22:13). He is therefore also "immortal," exempt from death. "Invisible" speaks of His essential spiritual nature (John 1:18; 4:24).

The "unapproachable light" God dwells in is His own glory. The apostle John wrote, "God is light; in him there is no darkness at all" (1 John 1:5). The psalmist wrote that He covers or "wraps" Himself with light as a garment (Psalm 104:2). He is "hid from our eyes" only by the brightness of His glory and the inability of our fallen souls to stand in the presence of such brilliant perfection. As the last line of the hymn states, "'Tis only the splendor of light hideth thee!'"

The first stanza of the hymn goes on to extol God as the "most blessed, most glorious, the Ancient of Days." That is one of the biblical names for God, stressing once again His eternality. "Ancient of Days" appears only three times in Scripture, all in Daniel 7. The Hebrew expression literally means, "one advanced in days." As a name for God it conveys the same truth as Job 36:26: "How great is God—beyond our understanding! The number of his years is past finding out." "Ancient of Days" also speaks of God's dignity and His wisdom. But lest anyone imagine God as a feeble geriatric, the hymn immediately reminds us that He is "almighty" and "victorious" as well.

The second stanza is a meditation on the truth of God's omnipotence. He is "unresting" because He never wearies and "unhasting" because He never needs to hurry. The expression "nor wanting, nor wasting" points out that He lacks nothing and that He has created nothing without a purpose.

In this stanza the songwriter evokes the image of light again to illustrate both the awesomeness and the subtlety of God's infinite power. He may be "silent as light," but like light, He is visible everywhere through the effects of His power.

The second half of the stanza praises the magnificence of His "justice like mountains"—mighty and majestic. God's justice is never merely the ruthless upholding of legal principle; it is a perfect justice tempered with goodness and love. So if mountains illustrate God's justice ("high soaring above"), His goodness and love are like clouds—loftier and even more awesome—giving the full picture an even richer beauty.

The hymn closes with a stanza that recaps and expands on the second line of the first verse, noting that the brilliance of God's splendor is such that even the angels surrounding His throne must cover their faces (Isaiah 6:2).

FROM OUT OF THE PAST

Bobbie Wolgemuth

WHAT WOULD BE THE MOST IMPORTANT THING that could come from a pastor's heart? This hymn was written by a pastor and preacher in the Free Church of Scotland. Being an esteemed church leader, he wanted to lead his parishioners into true worship. The object of that worship could hardly be described in earthly language, but Walter Chalmers Smith had the gift of poetry and was able to speak volumes of the character of his holy God with word-pictures.

Smith was a pastor for more than forty years and never relinquished the desire to lift up the character of God. Flowing from his pen were constant words that spoke of a preexistent "Ancient of Days" and a Creator God who gives life to both great and small. The poet reminds us that God is "almighty" and "victorious," yet is never in a hurry. He is "silent as light" and "invisible," yet pours out fountains of goodness and love. He is never in need of anything, does not waste anything, and never changes. How opposite from human characteristics is the immortal, only wise God.

The words of this hymn, when reflected upon, can bring us to the adoration and praise of the "Father of light." This is just what the author had in mind as he sought with pen and paper to find a way to lift the members of his own church to a vision of our awesome God. He knew that human needs begin to be met when people humble their hearts in reverent worship to the "Great Father of Glory."

Breathe on Me, Breath of God

EDWIN HATCH
1835-1899

Breathe on me, Breath of God,
fill me with life anew,
that I may love what thou dost love,
and do what thou wouldst do.

Breathe on me, Breath of God,
until my hears is pure,
until my will is one with thine,
to do and to endure.

Breathe on me, Breath of God,
till I am wholly thine,
until this earthly part of me
glows with thy fire divine.

Breathe on me, Breath of God,
so shall I never die,
but live with thee the perfect life
of thine eternity.

At the Heart of the Hymn

Joni Eareckson Tada

ی

Again Jesus said, "Peace be with you! As the Father has sent me, I am sending you." And with that he breathed on them and said, "Receive the Holy Spirit."

—JOHN 20:21-22

MY FRIEND JOHN IS BARELY MAKING IT. A severe neuromuscular disease is at the root of it all. When I went to visit him recently, I realized I couldn't stay long. John tires easily in his wheelchair. As if a feeding tube isn't enough, he is now facing the decision of whether or not to go on a ventilator. Breathing doesn't come easy for him. Maybe that's why, as a quadriplegic, I gain so much inspiration from being around John.

During my visit he said, "Sing for me." It was a simple enough request, so I launched into a round of happy-hearted hymns. I was surprised when I saw him mouth the words along with me.

"John, please don't tire yourself," I insisted. My friend, however, cannot resist a chance to enlarge his soul's capacity for God with the singing of a good hymn, and so he half-whispered, half-sang everything from "Climb, Climb Up Sunshine Mountain" to "All Hail the Power of Jesus' Name." By the close of our visit, he was exhausted. As John's eyes dropped to half-mast, I soothed him by singing:

Breathe on me, Breath of God,
Fill me with life anew,
That I may love what thou dost love,
And do what thou wouldst do.

It wasn't too many weeks later that I was rudely awakened in the middle of the night by a searing pain in the back of my neck. Try as I could, I was not able to squirm my shoulder into a comfortable position. (Remember, I'm paralyzed and can't move.) The clock read 2:00 A.M. and I didn't have the heart to wake up my husband, Ken. So I lay there in the dark, pushing away claustrophobic feelings. If only I could escape into sleep. If only morning would come. A quiet panic clutched at my throat, and I tried to fight it off by breathing deeply. Breathe in … breathe out … very slowly.

Suddenly it hit me. What I was struggling with for the moment, my friend John lives with every day. I then knew what to do about my pain and panic. I began softly singing to myself the same song that had quieted him. Except this time, it was a prayer for me. "Breathe on me, Breath of God." As the panic subsided, I thought about all the nights that John probably lies awake, fighting for each breath. I thought about the children I know with cystic fibrosis whose lungs are filling with fluid. I thought about those in circumstances more confining than mine. I asked the Lord to breathe peace, life, and His perspective into each person who came to mind. O God, stretch their soul's capacity for You, enlarge the heart of each one who is hurting.

John and others like him may not be able to do much more than half-whisper a hymn, but in so doing, they are increasing their capacity for God's peace and joy—it's enough to make life worth living, no matter how fragile one's life. That thought alone was enough to make me sigh, and before long I mumbled my last prayer and drifted off into a relaxed sleep.

Expending our breath on others like God does is the best prescription for peace.

In the Light of the Word

John MacArthur

⟡

JOHN 20 DESCRIBES HOW JESUS SUDDENLY APPEARED to His disciples in a closed room after His resurrection. While there, "he breathed on them and said, 'Receive the Holy Spirit'" (v. 22). There's an echo of that incident in this favorite and familiar hymn.

The impartation of the Holy Spirit was the means by which Christ empowered His apostles to serve Him after His ascension. In the Gospel accounts of Christ's earthly ministry, the disciples often seemed weak, timid, and easily confused. But after the Holy Spirit fell upon them at Pentecost, they were markedly different men. Peter, for example, who cowered before an accusing slave girl and denied knowing Christ on the eve of the Crucifixion, stepped forward at Pentecost and boldly proclaimed the Gospel to multitudes of potentially hostile unbelievers. The Holy Spirit made an immediate difference in all the disciples, infusing them with a holy boldness.

This hymn is a humble, prayerful recognition that no believer can ever achieve any measure of personal holiness or spiritual power apart from the gracious enabling of the Holy Spirit. The hymn is a plea for God to manifest and magnify the Spirit's transforming power—the "breath of God"—in the worshiper's life.

The imagery of the Holy Spirit as the breath of God is rooted in the earliest words of Genesis, where we read that at creation, "the Spirit of God was hovering over the waters" (1:2). The Hebrew word for "Spirit" can also mean both "wind" and "breath." So the imagery of Genesis 1:2 is that of God breathing on His creation, and the Holy Spirit Himself represents the breath of God.

The same imagery is carried throughout Scripture. Psalm 33:6 says, for example, "By the word of the Lord were the heavens made, their starry host by the breath of his mouth." Job 33:4 says, "The Spirit of God has made me; the breath of the Almighty gives me life."

Scripture pictures the creation of Adam in precisely these terms: "The Lord God formed the man from the dust of the ground and breathed into his nostrils the breath of life, and the man became a living being" (Genesis 2:7). Thus Scripture underscores the truth that all human life has its origin in the very breath of God. Man did not simply evolve from lower creatures; he alone of God's creatures had life breathed into him by God Himself.

But what our hymn has in view is the new creation—the rebirth of the sinner at salvation and the subsequent process of sanctification that progressively conforms us to the image of Christ. This, too, is a work of God's creative power, in which the Spirit of God awakens the spiritually dead sinner to new life (mentioned in the hymn's first stanza—"Fill me with life anew") and creates in him or her a new, obedient heart (cf. Ezekiel 36:26-27).

While recognizing and celebrating the work of the new creation as God's work, the hymn also reflects the reality that we are not yet what we ought to be. We are like Lazarus—raised by God from a state of death but still bound up and constricted in the grave-clothes of our own fallen human flesh (cf. John 11:44).

So the hymn is a prayer expressing a heartfelt longing for the image of Christ to be perfected in us through the constant outbreathing of the Holy Spirit. It explicitly pleads for holy desires and right behavior ("That I may love what thou dost love and do what thou wouldst do"), a cleansed heart ("until my heart is pure"), an obedient will ("Until my will is one with thine")—and ultimately total abandonment to God ("Till I am wholly thine"). Such requests constitute an implicit confession that the worshiper cannot, by sheer force of the human will, make himself be what he ought. Instead, we are utterly dependent on God's grace—dispensed to us through the ministry of the Holy Spirit, pictured here as the breath of God.

FROM OUT OF THE PAST

Bobbie Wolgemuth

E DWIN HATCH WAS A DISTINGUISHED LECTURER in Oxford, England, specializing in the rigorous study of early church history. For a brief time he was a professor of classics at Trinity College in Quebec, Canada. An Anglican minister, he was one of the few English theologians who won European recognition for original research. With all his head knowledge, however, he had the splendid gift of taking complex theological concepts and making them understandable to his students and parishioners. Many referred to his faith as being "simple and unaffected as a child."

The simple words "Breath on me, breath of God," penned first in a pamphlet when he was forty-three years old, entitled "Between Doubt and Prayer," barely reveal the brilliant scholarship and many accomplishments of the author.

For a man who could use any number of multisyllabic words to express profound truth, Edwin Hatch chose to fill this hymn-prayer with the most humble and uncomplicated words of a heart longing for God's touch. Often used as a prayer of consecration, the words penned by Edwin Hatch lead us to quietly plead, with childlike faith before the presence of our eternal Father, for the filling of the Holy Spirit.

O Love that Wilt Not Let Me Go

GEORGE MATHESON

1842-1906

O Love that wilt not let me go,
I rest my weary soul in thee;
I give thee back the life I owe,
that in thine ocean depths its flow
may richer, fuller be.

O Light that follow'st all my way,
I yield my flick'ring torch to thee;
my heart restores its borrowed ray,
that in thy sunshine's blaze its day
may brighter, fairer be.

O Joy that seekest me through pain,
I cannot close my heart to thee;
I trace the rainbow through the rain,
and feel the promise is not vain
that morn shall tearless be.

O Cross that liftest up my head,
I dare not ask to fly from thee;
I lay in dust life's glory dead,
and from the ground there blossoms red
life that shall endless be.

AT THE HEART OF THE HYMN

Joni Eareckson Tada

⌒

He heals the brokenhearted and binds up their wounds.

—PSALM 147:3

WHEN YOU'RE IN LOVE, your heart knows beyond a doubt that this is it. You grow faint, and your breathing becomes short just picturing the soft eyes and tender smile of the one you adore. Simply being in the same room together is a thrill. You ply that special person with questions just to hear the sound of his or her voice. And the thought of a kiss? An embrace? You all but melt. Lovers who speak of being "in love" lose themselves and then find themselves overwhelmed by something gloriously larger that possesses them. It's ecstatic.

Yet even this is meant to point us to a greater, more fulfilling joy. Although we cherish the glory in the one we love, we can easily forget that the glory is not in this special person so much as shining through him or her. C. S. Lewis described how we make the mistake of idolizing the one with whom we are smitten rather than reading the cues that keep whispering, "It's not me ... it's not in my eyes ... I'm only a reminder of Someone else."

Most of us never take this broad and glorious hint. We forget that the human soul was made to enjoy some object never given but only alluded to. We forget, that is, until our hearts become bruised or broken. Through a broken heart we find a Love that will not let us go. We collapse against His everlasting arms and realize that nothing—nothing—matches the sweetness of our Savior's superior love. In times of deepest affliction, I have inhaled the fragrance of His love and sung:

O Love that wilt not let me go,
I rest my weary soul in thee;
I give thee back the life I owe,
That in Thine ocean depths its flow
May richer, fuller be.

O Light that follow'st all my way,
I yield my flick'ring torch to thee;
My heart restores its borrowed ray,
That in thy sunshine's blaze its day
May brighter, fairer be.

Sometimes, in the middle of the night when I'm battling anxiety or weariness, an odd thing happens. I have often turned my head on the pillow and whispered, *O God, I miss You.* I believe that at such times my broken heart is seeking union with the Lord—not positional union, such as when we are first justified in Christ, but a union that is a warm, deep, and passionate melding of our heart with His.

Ah, but "If we suffer [with him], we shall also reign with him" (2 Timothy 2:12, KJV). And it will happen in the twinkling of an eye. We will be in the embrace of the Savior. The Lord's overcoming of the world will be a lifting of the curtain of our five senses, and we shall see Him and the whole universe in plain sight. At first the shock of joy may burn with the brilliant newness of being glorified, but in the next instant we will be at peace and feel at home, as though it were always this way, that we were born for such a place. A world of love, as Jonathan Edwards said.

Until then, we follow the lead of our Lover and lose ourselves in Him. We then find ourselves overwhelmed by Someone gloriously larger who grips our hearts. And it—rather, He—is ecstatic.

In the Light of the Word
John MacArthur

HERE'S ONE OF THE MOST MEANINGFUL and sublime of all hymns. George Matheson was a first-rate poet, and this is one of the finest and certainly the best-loved of all his works.

By his own testimony Matheson wrote this hymn while in a state of "the most severe mental suffering." But he called it "the quickest bit of work I ever did in my life." The words flowed from his pen, he said, as if the hymn had been dictated to him.

He wasn't claiming divine inspiration for his work, of course. But in the midst of such intense suffering, all his creative abilities, his poetic gifts, and every other faculty of mind and spirit were harnessed to express the passion of his heart, and this remarkably rich piece of poetry poured forth as the result.

Each stanza features one aspect of the poet's hope and comfort in the midst of his suffering. These are the eternal realities that brought him comfort in his anguish: God's love, the light of Scripture, the believer's joy, and the knowledge that our suffering produces glory. He takes them up a stanza at a time.

The first verse speaks of the divine love "that wilt not let me go." This is the sort of love God illustrated through the life of the prophet Hosea, who pursued his unfaithful wife and even bought her back from the slave market after she had spurned him and shamed him by playing the harlot. God's love for every believer is like Hosea's love for his wayward wife. It will not let us go. It pursued us and drew us to God before we ever even cared for Him (Romans 5:8). And having redeemed us, His love then won our hearts to Him. "We love God because he first loved us" (1 John 4:19).

Matheson portrayed that love as a soothing ocean of divine kindness in which he could rest his weary soul. Indeed, he recognized that it is every believer's bounden duty to abandon himself to that love ("I give thee back the life I owe") and let it radiate in our hearts (Romans 5:5)—"that in thine ocean depths its flow may richer, fuller be."

Stanza 2 features the "Light that follow'st all my way." The expression suggests that Matheson had in mind the light of divine truth, especially the Word of God, which is "a lamp to my feet and a light for my path" (Psalm 119:105). In that light the true believer's heart is refreshed and reignited, "restor[ing] its borrowed ray."

The third stanza speaks of joy—the true joy that every Christian can know even in the midst of the worst pain and sorrow. It is a heavenly joy that endures despite all earthly anguish. It is a deep and abiding joy that cannot be utterly snuffed out even by our bleakest woes. As believers we can always "trace the rainbow through the rain"—the rainbow being the symbol of God's promise. We can cling to God's promises for good even in life's most negative circumstances. After all, "we know that in all things"—even the unpleasant ones—"God works for the good of those who love him, who have been called according to his purpose" (Romans 8:28).

The final stanza mentions a cross. Matheson has in mind here not the cross of Christ, but the cross each believer is called to bear daily. "If anyone would come after me, he must deny himself and take up his cross daily and follow me"

(Luke 9:23). This stanza's theme is the inviolable spiritual principle Jesus teaches us in John 12:24-25: "Unless a kernel of wheat falls to the ground and dies, it remains only a single seed. But if it dies, it produces many seeds. The man who loves his life will lose it, while the man who hates his life in this world will keep it for eternal life."

Scripture often makes reference to the glory that follows suffering (cf. Romans 8:18; 1 Peter 4:13; 5:1). That promise of eternal glory is what makes it worthwhile to lay the glory of this life dead in the dust.

From Out of the Past

Bobbie Wolgemuth

GEORGE MATHESON, A BRILLIANT SCOTTISH SCHOLAR and preacher, was totally blind when he penned the words to "O Love That Wilt Not Let Me Go." Phrases like "O Light that follow'st all my way" reveal that he had learned to face his disability by inwardly looking ahead to the sunshine of God's blazing love and a brighter, fairer day.

It is no surprise that the focus of this hymn is the subject of love. It was written by a forty-year-old Matheson in his home on the day of his sister's wedding.

George was visually impaired as a young boy but was not totally blind until he was eighteen years old. In his teen years he fell in love. His fiancée, however, realizing he would soon be totally blind, broke their engagement. At eighteen years of age, despite a broken heart and a handicap that would have stopped most young people, George became a brilliant scholar and finished his studies at the

University and the Seminary of the Church of Scotland. His beloved sister assisted him in his theological endeavors by learning Latin, Greek, and Hebrew. Perhaps his devotion to her along with the memory of his own first love were the inspiration for writing "O Love That Wilt Not Let Me Go."

An actual account of the writing of this hymn was found in Dr. Matheson's own personal records. Something happened to him that he described as "known only to myself, and which caused me the most severe mental suffering." He went on to relate that he completed the hymn in five minutes under the most unusual anointing, and that it was the fruit of that suffering. "I had the impression rather of having it dictated to me by some inward voice than of working it out by myself. I have no natural gift of rhythm. All the other verses I have ever written are manufactured articles; this came like a dayspring from on high. I have never been able to gain once more the same fervor in verse."

Is it any wonder that the words of this hymn lift us beyond the realm of human love and help us "trace the rainbow through the rain"? We can begin every day with a note from the Creator of the Universe, who will not ever let us go.

Be Thou My Vision

IRISH TEXT TRANSLATED BY
MARY E. BYRNE
1880-1931

ANCIENT IRISH HYMN VERSIFIED BY
ELEANOR H. HULL
1860-1935

Be thou my vision, O Lord of my heart;
naught be all else to me, save that thou art—
thou my best thought by day or by night,
waking or sleeping, thy presence my light.

Be thou my wisdom and thou my true word;
I ever with thee and thou with me, Lord;
thou my great Father, I thy true son;
thou in me dwelling, and I with thee one.

Be thou my battle shield, sword for my fight;
be thou my dignity, thou my delight,
thou my soul's shelter, thou my high tow'r:
raise thou me heav'n-ward, O Pow'r of my pow'r.

Riches I heed not, nor man's empty praise,
thou mine inheritance, now and always:
thou and thou only, first in my heart,
High King of heaven, my treasure thou art.

High King of heaven, my victory won,
may I reach heaven's joys, O bright heav'n's Sun!
Heart of my own heart, whatever befall,
still be my vision, O Ruler of all.

At the Heart of the Hymn

Joni Eareckson Tada

ࠩ

But whatever was to my profit I now consider loss for the sake of Christ.

—PHILIPPIANS 3:7

THE HILLS ABOVE BELFAST WERE GREEN with the emerald color of spring and fresh from the damp sea-blown breezes. It was my first trip to Ulster in the northern part of Ireland, and I felt at home. I wondered if my grandmother, whom I had never met, walked these hills above the North Sea. Did she amble among the hillside flowers, gathering Irish Bells in her apron? Did she walk the winding paths and sit at the feet of ancient trees lining the cliffs? Did she face the wind and sea and, like me, sing the old Irish hymn:

Be thou my vision, O Lord of my heart;
Naught be all else to me, save that Thou art—
Thou my best thought by day or by night,
Waking or sleeping, thy presence my light.

I wish I had known my grandmother, Anna Verona Cacey. They tell me she was a saint. She had immigrated to America in the late 1800s, met and married my grandfather, William Milton Eareckson, and raised four rough-and-tumble boys, all of whom were athletic and fun-loving. Anna Verona's prayers kept them in line, especially young Johnny whose job it was to hitch the horses to the wagon and shovel coal into the neighborhood cellars each day before dawn. It wasn't an easy job. It was even tougher to keep the boys' focus on Christ and church activities as sounds of the Roaring 20s echoed through the west end of Baltimore.

Years later a wistful smile would cross my father's face and his eyes would dampen as he'd recall, "There were many a time my brothers and I would argue about whose turn it was to go down into the basement to bring up the coal. Before you knew it, we'd turn to see Mother coming up the steps in her long skirts hauling that heavy bucket. Then there were nights I'd come home late from the YMCA or from Boys Brigade at church and find my mother sitting by the coal stove, afghan over her knees with her Bible on her lap. I knew she had been praying for me."

And probably singing too. As I understand it, my grandmother had the lilt of an Irish songbird, and hymns from her homeland always filled the Eareckson household with praises to God.

Little wonder Anna Verona captured my thoughts as I sat on the hill above Belfast. She is a part of the beauty and history of this gloriously green emerald isle, just like "Be Thou My Vision." I'm so grateful to God for my grandmother's vision, her Spirit-inspired ability to see the world, her world, as God saw it. With a focus fastened on the Lord Jesus, she was able to see the invisible—a son named Johnny who would grow into a noble man of fine character and tender heart, passing on the love of Christ to his daughter … his namesake.

May God give me the grace to see the world as it should be. May I keep the vision.

High King of heaven, my victory won,
May I reach heaven's joys, O bright heav'n's Sun!
Heart of my own heart, whatever befall,
Still be my vision, O Ruler of all.

In the Light of the Word

John MacArthur

*T*HIS IS THE MOST ANCIENT HYMN in most of today's familiar evangelical hymnbooks. It dates back to the Irish church of the eighth century. Despite the antiquity of the hymn, the Irish church was already at least three centuries old when it was written. St. Patrick had been converted in Ireland when he was sent there to be a slave in the early fifth century. He escaped slavery and was ordained to the ministry somewhere on the European continent before returning to Ireland to begin his great missionary work there in 432. "Be Thou My Vision" seems to have originated in Ireland some 300 years later.

So this hymn came out of a long-established church with deep theological roots, and the simple profundity of its message reflects that. In places the poetry of the English translation may be a bit difficult to follow. The second line of the hymn in particular ("Naught be all else to me, save that thou art") sounds a bit jarring and archaic to the modern ear. But to paraphrase that line, it is a prayer for God to take away our esteem for everything but Himself, so that everything we desire is everything He is.

In fact, that second line perfectly sums up the whole meaning of the hymn. It is a plea for God to establish Himself as the worshiper's chief object of desire and affection. Implicit in the plea is a recognition of God's sovereignty over the human heart. The writer of this hymn (whose name is lost in the Celtic church tradition) was acknowledging that God's own gracious enablement is necessary before the human heart can have an appropriate passion for God. And so he prays that his spiritual eyes would be filled with a vision of God, so that his desires would never be diverted to lesser things such as earthly riches or man's empty praise.

This hymn is a classic example of the deep piety that usually permeates the best of early and medieval church writings. It is a classic devotional prayer, including several allusions to Scripture. For example, the second line of the fourth stanza ("Thou mine inheritance, now and always") is a reference to Psalm 16:5 ("The Lord is the portion of my inheritance and my cup," NASB) and Psalm 73:26 ("My flesh and my heart may fail, but God is the strength of my heart and my portion forever").

Although the message is devotional rather than theological, the theology that is featured in the hymn is impeccable. The second stanza, for example, extols the all-sufficiency of God and His revelation as the believer's only true Word and wisdom. It also celebrates the inviolable security of the believer's relationship with the Almighty ("I ever with thee and thou with me, Lord"). That stanza also notes the multiple layers of relationship between believers and their God, who is not only their Father but who also indwells them and is one with them by spiritual union.

The doctrine of the believer's eternal security is also clearly implied in the hymn's affirmation that God is our inheritance "now and always." And yet the closing stanza also acknowledges the balance of that truth: The perseverance of the believer is an essential aspect of that security. And so the final verse is a prayer for the grace that enables us to persevere.

Again there is a powerful presupposition underlying this petition. It is the clear recognition that God is the One who graciously enables and assures our perseverance in the faith. "You … are kept by the power of God through faith for salvation ready to be revealed in the last time" (1 Peter 1:4-5, NKJV). And so the hymn closes with an expectant hope of ultimate victory, punctuated with the same plea that began the hymn, as the believer rests in the confidence that "whatever befall," God will continue the good work He has begun in us (Philippians 1:6).

FROM OUT OF THE PAST
Bobbie Wolgemuth

B E THOU MY VISION," originally written as an Irish poem, was discovered by a researcher and writer in Dublin, Ireland, Mary E. Byrne, who worked for the Board of Intermediate Education. It was not put into verse form for singing until a history and literature writer, Eleanor H. Hull, rewrote it and put it in her work, *The Poem Book of the Gael*. The words were then set to the melody of a traditional Irish tune.

It is interesting to note that two women were so touched by the words of this poem that they studied it, preserved it, and finally shaped it into a poetic format for the ages. The words speak of God's tenderness as "Lord of my heart," "my great Father," "mine inheritance," and "my best thought by day or by night." This gentle insight from a woman's heart leads us to yearn for the intimacy with God that they treasured.

The other references to God as the "High King of heaven" and "O Bright heav'n's Sun" also lift up the Object of our worship.

In churches all across Ireland today, this hymn is frequently used as the opening song for worship services. The words that lift the people to praise, giving them confidence in their victorious High King, have become a theme song for the church.

My Faith Has Found a Resting Place

LIDIE H. EDMUNDS

NINETEENTH CENTURY

My faith has found a resting place,
from guilt my soul is freed;
I trust the ever-living One,
his wounds for me shall plead.

CHORUS:

I need no other argument,
I need no other plea,
it is enough that Jesus died,
and that he died for me.

Enough for me that Jesus saves,
this ends my fear and doubt;
a sinful soul I come to him,
he'll never cast me out.

CHORUS

My heart is leaning on the Word,
the written Word of God:
salvation by my Savior's name,
salvation thro' his blood.

CHORUS

My great Physician heals the sick,
the lost he came to save;
for me his precious blood he shed,
for me his life he gave.

CHORUS

AT THE HEART OF THE HYMN

Joni Eareckson Tada

乀

*In that day the Root of Jesse will stand as a banner for
the peoples; the nations will rally to him, and his place
of rest will be glorious.*

—ISAIAH 11:10

WHEN MY FRIENDS FRANCIE AND JUDY and I travel together, it means flying out from Los Angeles early, arriving at our destination late, hitting the hotel room later, unpacking fast, sleeping faster, awaking to coffee and Special K cereal, scrambling to get ready, grabbing our things, and heading out the door. Almost.

Before we leave for the morning's appointments and interviews—a breakfast at which I'm to speak or a visit to a rehab center—we pause. Judy sits on the edge of the bed next to her briefcase, and Francie reads that day's devotional. We pray and after "Amens," Judy stands up, virtually salutes, and announces with great enthusiasm, "Let's go slay dragons!" That's the way it usually goes.

On my last trip back east we did something different. I always photocopy a hymn and have Francie place it in the front of my speaking notebook. That way, if there's a lull in the schedule, such as an airport delay or a long van ride, we can pass the time by memorizing the verses. On the first morning we were in Boston, I piped up, "Hey, girls, how about if we sing the 'trip hymn' for devotions this morning?" Judy checked her watch; we had time. Francie got the speaking notebook, and she and Judy crowded around me in the bathroom and sang:

*My faith has found a resting place
From guilt my soul is freed;*

I trust the ever-living One,
His wounds for me shall plead.
I need no other argument, I need no other plea,
It is enough that Jesus died, and that he died for me.

"You're singing that wrong," Judy said to me.

"No, I'm not."

"Then why are you singing a quarter note here?" Francie asked, pointing to the half note in the fifth measure.

"'Cause that's the way I learned it. Let me see that …" I squinted at the sheet music.

"You've just gotta prove you're right," one of them said, getting a bit testy.

"No . . ." My voice began to rise. "I just want to see how it reads."

"Yeah, yeah, we know …"

It was beginning to get steamy in the bathroom. "Honestly, I just want to read the stupid music," I insisted, half-serious and half-laughing.

At that point Judy (who, incidentally, wouldn't know a whole note from a half) leaned in and pointed to something more important than any old note of music, saying, "I need no other argument, Joni … Let's quit this and get on with the day." With that, the air suddenly cleared. We grabbed our things, took the Do Not Disturb sign off the door handle, and left the room. Our faith had found a resting place—agreement around God and His mission.

The girls went ahead of me to catch the elevator, humming and filling the hallway with "I need no other argument, I need no other plea, it is enough that Jesus died, and that he died for me."

And I was careful to hum the half note.

In the Light of the Word

John MacArthur

⟨⟩

THIS EXCELLENT GOSPEL SONG IS A TESTIMONY about trusting Christ alone for salvation. The song is by no means complex or advanced theology, but it is a profound statement of faith nonetheless: "It is enough that Jesus died, and that he died for me."

That final line of the refrain speaks of the utter sufficiency of Christ's atoning death to purchase full pardon for sinners who look to Him alone for their salvation. He paid the price of the believer's sin in full. He wrought a complete redemption. Nothing needs to be added—indeed, nothing can possibly add value to that which is infinitely precious already. So, real faith in Christ is by definition faith in Him alone.

All the punishment for our sin was borne by Him; all the merit we need to please God is supplied by Him as well. Just as our guilt was imputed to Him, so His righteousness is imputed to us (2 Corinthians 5:21). What more could possibly be added to that?

In other words, the believer contributes nothing meritorious to the process of redemption. That simple, central truth of the Gospel is too often forgotten. It is a seemingly irrepressible human tendency to think that we can and must do something to atone for our own sins. Every religion ever invented by man pretends to tell people how they can better themselves, make up for the wrongs they have done, free themselves from their own sin, and make themselves acceptable to God. True biblical religion alone teaches that God Himself provides for sinners everything they need to be reconciled to Him.

And this song is the heart-cry of someone who understood that truth. "My faith has found a resting place." The true object of our faith is neither "device nor creed" (traditional rendering). Rituals, religious apparatus, earthly organizations, and man-made creeds are all inappropriate objects of faith. The one true ground of our trust and hope is none other than the Person of Christ, whose real flesh-and-blood wounds are objective proof that He has completely paid for the sins of His people. The true believer needs "no other argument … no other plea."

As the second stanza points out, when our faith rests in Christ, "this ends … fear and doubt." Romans 8:1 gives the reason for such confidence before God: "There is therefore now no condemnation for those who are in Christ Jesus."

The believer is secure in Christ as well: "He'll never cast me out." That, of course, is an allusion to the truth of John 6:37, where Jesus promised, "Him that cometh to me I will in no wise cast out" (KJV).

The third stanza is an expression of absolute confidence in "the written Word of God," the only infallible source of everything we know about Christ and His promises—especially the promise of "salvation by my Savior's name, salvation thro' his blood."

The closing stanza of this song follows up on the idea of blood-bought salvation. It opens with an allusion to Christ's own description of His mission: "The Son of man came to seek and to save what was lost" (Luke 19:10). And it returns immediately to the theme of Christ's giving His blood for our redemption.

It's interesting to note how many of the nineteenth-century hymns and gospel songs expressly mention the blood of Jesus. They were deliberately stressing the truth that Christ's violent death was an appeasement of divine justice and a satisfaction of God's holy wrath against sin. That era had seen the growth of a spurious brand of Christianity that tried to downplay the sacrificial work of Christ and emphasize only His moral teachings. These hymns and gospel songs stressed that apart from the pouring out of Christ's lifeblood as a sacrifice for sins, there is no hope and no salvation for sinners.

From Out of the Past

Bobbie Wolgemuth

⁀

OFTEN THE HYMNS WE SING began as poetry or verses penned by believers who wished to express some deep truth they had discovered in their own Christian walk.

We know very little about the writer of the words to this song, other than her name, Lidie H. Edmunds, attached to the words when it first appeared in the 1891 hymnal *Songs of Joy and Gladness*. We also know that the tune ultimately attached to her words was an old Norwegian melody.

Even without knowing her, when we study the words, we see the heart of Lidie Edmunds. We see a woman full of trust and dependence and assurance. Her reflection on God as the Great Physician who heals the sick of body and soul sounds like it could have been an intercessory prayer for a loved one, or perhaps for herself. For the believer who is struggling with doubt and fear, she gives the antidote that moved her from frailty to faith: Depend on sacred Scripture, or as she put it, "the written Word of God."

The comfort she affirmed was that "the ever-living One" would plead her case and never cast her out. She learned of this Savior through the study of her Bible, because she leaned "on the Word." It would not collapse. It was her resting place, in spite of device or creed. In every circumstance, no argument was necessary. God's Word would be enough.

The Hymns
WORDS AND MUSIC

O Worship the King

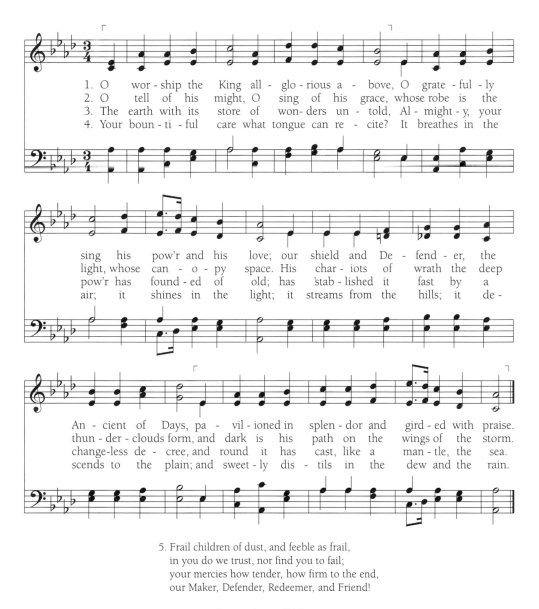

1. O wor-ship the King all - glo-rious a - bove, O grate-ful - ly
2. O tell of his might, O sing of his grace, whose robe is the
3. The earth with its store of won-ders un - told, Al - might-y, your
4. Your boun-ti-ful care what tongue can re - cite? It breathes in the

sing his pow'r and his love; our shield and De - fend-er, the
light, whose can - o - py space. His char - iots of wrath the deep
pow'r has found-ed of old; has 'stab-lished it fast by a
air; it shines in the light; it streams from the hills; it de -

An - cient of Days, pa - vil - ioned in splen-dor and gird-ed with praise.
thun - der-clouds form, and dark is his path on the wings of the storm.
change-less de - cree, and round it has cast, like a man - tle, the sea.
scends to the plain; and sweet-ly dis - tils in the dew and the rain.

5. Frail children of dust, and feeble as frail,
in you do we trust, nor find you to fail;
your mercies how tender, how firm to the end,
our Maker, Defender, Redeemer, and Friend!

6. O measureless Might! Ineffable Love!
While angels delight to hymn you above,
the humbler creation, though feeble their lays,
with true adoration shall lisp to your praise.

Based on Psalm 104
Robert Grant, 1833
Mod.

LYONS 10.10.11.11.
Johann Michael Haydn, 1737-1806
Arr. in William Gardner's *Sacred Melodies*, 1815

A Mighty Fortress Is Our God

and armed with cru - el hate, on earth is not his e - qual.
from age to age the same, and he must win the bat - tle.
for lo! his doom is sure; one lit - tle word shall fell him.
God's truth a - bid - eth still; his king - dom is for - ev - er.

Based on Psalm 46
Martin Luther, 1529
Tr. by Frederick H. Hedge, 1853

EIN' FESTE BURG 8.7.8.7.6.6.6.6.7.
Martin Luther, 1529

Man of Sorrows! What a Name

1. Man of Sor - rows! what a name for the Son of God, who came
2. Bear - ing shame and scoff - ing rude, in my place con - demned he stood,
3. Guilt - y, vile, and help - less, we; spot - less Lamb of God was he;
4. Lift - ed up was he to die, "It is fin - ished!" was his cry;
5. When he comes, our glo - rious King, all his ran - somed home to bring,

ru - ined sin - ners to re - claim: Hal - le - lu - jah! what a Sav - ior!
sealed my par - don with his blood: Hal - le - lu - jah! what a Sav - ior!
full a - tone - ment! can it be? Hal - le - lu - jah! what a Sav - ior!
now in heav'n ex - alt - ed high: Hal - le - lu - jah! what a Sav - ior!
then a - new this song we'll sing: Hal - le - lu - jah! what a Sav - ior!

Philip P. Bliss, 1875

HALLELUJAH! WHAT A SAVIOR! 7.7.7.8.
Philip P. Bliss, 1875

It Is Well with My Soul

1. When peace, like a riv - er, at - tend - eth my way, when sor - rows like
2. Though Sa - tan should buf - fet, though tri - als should come, let this blest as -
3. My sin — O the bliss of this glo - ri - ous thought!—my sin, not in
4. O Lord, haste the day when the faith shall be sight, the clouds be rolled

sea bil - lows roll; what - ev - er my lot, thou hast taught me to say,
sur - ance con - trol, that Christ has re - gard - ed my help - less es - tate,
part, but the whole, is nailed to the cross and I bear it no more;
back as a scroll, the trump shall re - sound and the Lord shall de - scend,

REFRAIN

"It is well, it is well with my soul."
and has shed his own blood for my soul. It is well
praise the Lord, praise the Lord, O my soul! It is well
"E - ven so" — it is well with my soul.

with my soul; it is well, it is well with my soul.
with my soul;

Horatio G. Spafford, 1873

VILLE DU HAVRE 11.8.11.9.ref.
Philip P. Bliss, 1875

Immortal, Invisible, God Only Wise

1. Im - mor - tal, in - vis - i - ble, God on - ly wise,
2. Un - rest - ing, un - hast - ing and si - lent as light,
3. Great Fa - ther of glo - ry, pure Fa - ther of light,

in light in - ac - ces - si - ble hid from our eyes,
nor want - ing, nor wast - ing, thou rul - est in might;
thine an - gels a - dore thee, all veil - ing their sight;

most bless - ed, most glo - rious, the An - cient of Days,
thy jus - tice like moun - tains high soar - ing a - bove
all praise we would ren - der; O help us to see

al - might - y, vic - to - rious, thy great name we praise.
thy clouds which are foun - tains of good - ness and love.
'tis on - ly the splen - dor of light hid - eth thee!

Walter Chalmers Smith, 1867

JOANNA (or ST. DENIO) 11.11.11.11.
Traditional Welsh hymn melody

I Know Whom I Have Believed

1. I know not why God's won-drous grace to me he has made known,
2. I know not how this sav-ing faith to me he did im-part,
3. I know not how the Spir-it moves, con-vinc-ing men of sin,
4. I know not what of good or ill may be re-served for me,
5. I know not when my Lord may come, at night or noon-day fair,

nor why, un-wor-thy, Christ in love re-deemed me for his own.
nor how be-liev-ing in his Word wrought peace with-in my heart.
re-veal-ing Je-sus through the Word, cre-at-ing faith in him.
of wea-ry ways or gold-en days, be-fore his face I see.
nor if I'll walk the vale with him, or "meet him in the air."

REFRAIN

But "I know whom I have be-liev-ed, and am per-suad-ed that he is

a-ble to keep that which I've com-mit-ted un-to him a-gainst that day."

Daniel W. Whittle, 1883

EL NATHAN C.M. ref.
James McGranahan, 1883

O Sacred Head, Now Wounded

1. O sa-cred Head, now wound-ed, with grief and shame weighed down;
2. What thou, my Lord, hast suf-fered was all for sin-ners' gain:
3. What lan-guage shall I bor-row to thank thee, dear-est Friend,

now scorn-ful-ly sur-round-ed with thorns, thine on-ly crown;
mine, mine was the trans-gres-sion, but thine the dead-ly pain.
for this, thy dy-ing sor-row, thy pit-y with-out end?

O sa-cred Head, what glo-ry, what bliss till now was thine!
Lo, here I fall, my Sav-ior! 'Tis I de-serve thy place;
O make me thine for-ev-er; and should I faint-ing be,

Yet, though de-spised and gor-y, I joy to call thee mine.
look on me with thy fa-vor, vouch-safe to me thy grace.
Lord, let me nev-er, nev-er out-live my love to thee.

Bernard of Clairvaux, 1091-1153
Tr. by Paul Gerhardt, 1656
Tr. by James W. Alexander, 1830

PASSION CHORALE 7.6.7.6.D.
Hans Leo Hassler, 1601
Arr. by Johann Sebastian Bach, 1729

O the Deep, Deep Love of Jesus!

1. O the deep, deep love of Je - sus! Vast, un - mea - sured,
2. O the deep, deep love of Je - sus! Spread his praise from
3. O the deep, deep love of Je - sus! Love of ev - 'ry

bound - less, free; roll - ing as a might - y o - cean
shore to shore; how he lov - eth, ev - er lov - eth,
love the best: 'tis an o - cean vast of bless - ing,

in its full - ness o - ver me. Un - der - neath me, all a - round me,
chang - eth nev - er, nev - er - more; how he watch - es o'er his loved ones,
'tis a ha - ven sweet of rest. O the deep, deep love of Je - sus!

is the cur - rent of thy love; lead - ing on - ward,
died to call them all his own; how for them he
'Tis a heav'n of heav'ns to me; and it lifts me

lead - ing home - ward, to thy glo - rious rest a - bove.
in - ter - ced - eth, watch - eth o'er them from the throne.
up to glo - ry, for it lifts me up to thee.

Samuel Trevor Francis, 1834-1925

EBENEZER (or TON-Y-BOTEL) 8.7.8.7.D.
Thomas John Williams, 1890

Breathe on Me, Breath of God

1. Breathe on me, Breath of God, fill me with life a - new,
2. Breathe on me, Breath of God, un - til my heart is pure,
3. Breathe on me, Breath of God, till I am whol - ly thine,
4. Breathe on me, Breath of God, so shall I nev - er die,

that I may love what thou dost love, and do what thou wouldst do.
un - til my will is one with thine, to do and to en - dure.
un - til this earth - ly part of me glows with thy fire di - vine.
but live with thee the per - fect life of thine e - ter - ni - ty

Edwin Hatch, 1878

TRENTHAM S.M.
Robert Jackson, 1888

Be Thou My Vision

1. Be thou my vi - sion, O Lord of my heart; naught be all else to me, save that thou art— thou my best thought by day or by night, wak - ing or sleep - ing, thy pres - ence my light.

2. Be thou my wis - dom, and thou my true word; I ev - er with thee and thou with me, Lord; thou my great Fa - ther, I thy true son; thou in me dwell - ing, and I with thee one.

3. Be thou my bat - tle shield, sword for my fight; be thou my dig - ni - ty, thou my de - light, thou my soul's shel - ter, thou my high tow'r: raise thou me heav'n-ward, O Pow'r of my pow'r.

4. Rich - es I heed not, nor man's emp - ty praise, thou mine in - her - i - tance, now and al - ways: thou and thou on - ly, first in my heart, High King of heav - en, my trea - sure thou art.

5. High King of heav - en, my vic - to - ry won, may I reach heav - en's joys, O bright heav'n's Sun! Heart of my own heart, what - ev - er be - fall, still be my vi - sion, O Rul - er of all.

Ancient Irish poem, ca. 8th cent.
Tr. by Mary E. Byrne, 1905
Versified by Eleanor H. Hull, 1912

SLANE 10.10.10.10.
Traditional Irish melody
Arr. by David Evans, 1927

Tune arr. © 1927 from the *Revised Church Hymnary* by permission of Oxford University Press

O Love That Wilt Not Let Me Go

1. O Love that wilt not let me go, I rest my
2. O Light that fol-low'st all my way, I yield my
3. O Joy that seek-est me through pain, I can-not
4. O Cross that lift-est up my head, I dare not

wea - ry soul in thee; I give thee back the life I owe,
flick - 'ring torch to thee; my heart re - stores its bor - rowed ray,
close my heart to thee; I trace the rain - bow through the rain,
ask to fly from thee; I lay in dust life's glo - ry dead,

that in thine o - cean depths its flow may rich - er, full - er be.
that in thy sun - shine's blaze its day may bright - er, fair - er be.
and feel the prom - ise is not vain that morn shall tear - less be.
and from the ground there blos - soms red life that shall end - less be.

George Matheson, 1882

ST. MARGARET 8.8.8.8.6.
Albert L Peace, 1885

My Faith Has Found a Resting Place

1. My faith has found a rest-ing place, from guilt my soul is freed;
2. E-nough for me that Je-sus saves, this ends my fear and doubt;
3. My heart is lean-ing on the Word, the writ-ten Word of God:
4. My great Phy-si-cian heals the sick, the lost he came to save;

I trust the ev-er-liv-ing One, his wounds for me shall plead.
a sin-ful soul I come to him, he'll nev-er cast me out.
sal-va-tion by my Sav-ior's name, sal-va-tion thro' his blood.
for me his pre-cious blood he shed, for me his life he gave.

REFRAIN

I need no oth-er ar-gu-ment, I need no oth-er plea,

it is e-nough that Je-sus died, and that he died for me.

Lidie H. Edmunds, 1891
Alt. 1990

LANDAS C.M.ref.
André Gretry, 1741-1831
Arr. by William J. Kirkpatrick, 1891